with Pleasure

MANAGING TRAUMA TRIGGERS FOR MORE VIBRANT SEX AND RELATIONSHIPS

AUGUST MCLAUGHLIN & JAMILA DAWSON, LMFT

CHICAGO
REVIEW
PRESS

Published by Chicago Review Press, Incorporated
814 North Franklin Street
Chicago, Illinois 60610
ISBN 978-1-64160-503-8

Library of Congress Control Number: 2021909510

Cover and Interior design: Sadie Teper

Printed in the United States of America
5 4 3 2 1

Jamila:

For my ancestors and for those who will come after me,

August:

For anyone feeling lost or alone,

And

for you.

Contents

About This Book

First things first. No matter your age, gender, or type of trauma you've endured, you are welcome here. There is no particular type of trauma you have to have experienced for this book to support you. If you are trauma-comparing, wondering whether what you've gone through is "bad" enough to deserve support (*But other people have it so much worse!*), or think that the intense magnitude of your situation or struggle to cope somehow disqualifies you, please set those thoughts aside. We are all worthy of support and pleasure.

As for who we, your authors/fellow students/guides, are, Jamila Dawson, LMFT, is a pleasure-based, trauma-informed sex therapist who serves folks of all genders and orientations who are looking to shed shame and disconnection and create new sexual and relationship possibilities. August McLaughlin is a journalist, author of *Girl Boner*, and host and producer of *Girl Boner Radio*, a podcast about sexual empowerment created through a femme lens for everyone. We're both trauma-informed sex educators who prioritize social justice as well, and we are so grateful that you're here.

Throughout this book, you'll hear from people who've experienced trauma-related trigger flares because of sexual assault, domestic violence, losing loved ones, intergenerational trauma, and harmful societal or religious messaging. You'll hear from someone whose trauma happened so early in life the survivor doesn't remember it, and from those who couldn't stop recalling far more details than they would have liked, folks who are early in their paths of healing and those who've embraced healing practices and supports for decades. Some featured survivors have been diagnosed with depression, anxiety, or post-traumatic stress disorder. Others have never been diagnosed with or met the criteria for these conditions. All are equally valid.

You matter. Your feelings matter. And there is not a single ounce of shame in struggling. You are here, reading these pages and desiring to do important, worthy work toward healing. For that intent alone, you are phenomenal and brave.

THE LAYOUT

Each chapter of *With Pleasure* is titled with a phrase or question common among survivors who are feeling stuck in the grasp of trauma. Many of these thoughts crop up in our darkest moments. We might find ourselves obsessing over, shrouding in secrecy, or endlessly googling these thoughts in search of relief. For the sake of organizing this book, these phrases include:

"Why is this happening to me?"

"What is happening to me?"

"How can I stop this?"

"I need help."

"I am such a problem."

"Healing is taking too long."

"They don't understand."

"How can I get my life back?"

"Should I forgive? If so, how?"

"Dang it, I thought I was healed."

Each chapter includes a blend of true stories, Jamila's expert insight, relevant research findings, and practical tips and takeaways, all with special focus on reclaiming pleasure, sexual and otherwise, and navigating intimate relationships. Many chapters include prompts for suggested activities. You'll also find a simple grounding exercise between each chapter. These quick activities are meant to help bring you back to the present moment when you feel triggered. Please jump to these activities any time they may be helpful.

NOTES ABOUT THE LANGUAGE AND CONTENT

Since we began working on this book, the word *triggered* has been increasingly co-opted by people who prioritize making fun of anyone with differing political views, versus understanding people's unique challenges and experiences across all intersections of life. When we use the term *triggered*, we're not talking about the casual "this might be a bit unpleasant to read"–type warnings prevalent on social media. Such warnings may be helpful for survivors, but when trigger-related terms are used to describe benign or casual matters or, worse, to ridicule people, it can feel diminishing to someone in the throes of trauma. And in some cases, adding trigger warnings ends up defeating the purpose.

The term *triggered* is increasingly common in everyday conversation, which on the one hand is a good thing because discussing challenges with mental wellness can lead to reducing stigma and shame and make it easier for people to reach out for help because they can recognize that they're in distress. On the other hand, it's important to use the word correctly. As we've been seeing, *triggered* is a word that is particularly vulnerable to being misunderstood and used in ways that minimize or obscure its true meaning. We use *triggered* to describe a mind/somatic response. When we are triggered, we are physically unable to recognize and remain in the present moment. As far as our minds and bodies are concerned, we are caught in a moment in which our fight, flight, freeze, or fawn response has taken over and our ability to figure out what is happening and what to do (executive functioning) is inaccessible or severely compromised. When we are triggered, the mind/body response is really happening and our nervous system is valiantly attempting to protect us both physically and emotionally. This experience can be terrifying and confusing and, too often, people feel intense shame for what they perceive as or have been told indicates being "out of control" or "too sensitive."

It's important to know that when we're triggered, there is nothing to be ashamed of. Your body is doing its absolute best to protect and defend itself to ensure your survival into the next moment. It's quite incredible. And yet, being at the whim of flashbacks or other internal feelings of disruption is not a way to live our lives to their fullest.

One of the reasons we believe the word *triggered* has become so misused and abused is because, as a society that is individualistic and privileges pain over pleasure ("No pain, no gain!"), we don't have shared cultural language for the different aspects of pain. Because being triggered is such a specific experience, we want to offer you freedom to use other words to describe trauma responses you may experience in your life or even as you read this book. What's important is that you deepen your emotional vocabulary and create language to place around your own experience, so that you not only begin to have awareness of your distress but also, over time, become attuned to your magnificent capacity for all kinds of pleasure.

We also sometimes use the term *activated* as a synonym of *triggered*. While *triggered* is arguably the most common term used for these episodes, some people find it too violent. Meanwhile, others feel the term is appropriately violent, given the kind of feelings and experiences the episodes bring. We welcome you to use whatever terminology feels best in your own life. Similarly, we use the word *survivor* when referring to someone who has endured or continues to manage trauma. If you feel more empowered or comfortable using words like *victim* or simply *person* at times or indefinitely, please continue using those words.

As much as possible, we have respected the words and descriptors used by each interviewee within their story. If a term or phrase used to describe their situation troubles you in any way, we invite you to extend grace to them, come up with your own language, and/or skip to a different place. In honoring your own reactions, you can take what is useful and leave behind what doesn't help in any given moment.

Certain minor details, such as some names and other identifiers, have been changed for the sake of privacy. All of the stories are true, to the best of our own and contributors' knowledge and memory.

The content of *With Pleasure* is best suited for people who have endured some type of trauma and continue to grapple with the aftereffects but aren't currently in acute life-threatening depths of a root cause. If you're currently going through trauma, such as domestic violence, this book may shed light on useful information, but it won't help you thrive in a dangerous situation. In other words, this book is not a substitute for medical or crisis care, nor is it a substitute for therapy.

This book also cannot, unfortunately, eliminate the destructive and dehumanizing systems—such as systemic racism, classism, ableism, transphobia, xenophobia, ageism, biphobia, heterosexism, and sizeism—that fuel trauma. That said, we hope that by bringing more light to these factors, survivors and their loved ones alike will gain understanding and validation, and potentially help chip away at these types of oppression in whatever ways we individually and collectively can.

———

If you feel you may be in harm's way, here are a few immediate and
   anonymous resources for support:
BlackLine, for BIPoC: (800) 604-5841
National Eating Disorders Association Hotline: (800) 931-2237
National Sexual Assault Hotline: (800) 656-4673
National Suicide Prevention Hotline: (800) 273-8255
The Gay, Lesbian, Bisexual and Transgender National Hotline:
   (888) 843-4564
For the Crisis Text Line, text START to 741-741.

WHAT YOU WILL NOT FIND IN THIS BOOK
Graphic, Gratuitous Details About Traumatic Experiences
While we've included basic details about many survivors' trauma for context and understanding, we have avoided explicit details for the sake of reader sensitivity. Even so, we can't always predict what might trigger us and even basic information may feel intense at times. Please take best care of yourself, stepping away or skipping any parts that feel too difficult. (And again, please keep those grounding exercises handy.)

All of the Answers or a Cookie-Cutter Plan
This book is not the kind of self-help book that prescribes a step-by-step

plan intended to work for everyone. Consider it a companion you can turn to for support, knowledge, encouragement, resources, and clinical and survivors' expert insight. We believe that you are the expert of your own life, and we want to help create space for and facilitate additional healing, growth, pleasure, and vibrancy in your life, however that may look for you. All of our paths are unique. Our hope is that *With Pleasure* will help you find your way to or further ongoing healing, whether you use it on its own or in tandem with one or more treatment or management modalities.

HOW TO USE THIS BOOK

Feel free to read this book straight through, from cover to cover, or skip to whatever sections feel most relevant or helpful to you at any given time. If you feel anxious or triggered by anything you read or in your daily life and wish to re-center yourself and feel calmer, jump to one of the grounding exercises between chapters. Choose one that most appeals or feels more helpful in any given moment, and consider bookmarking your favorites. These exercises are intentionally simple and take little time to engage in. We also invite you to come up with your own grounding practices, if you feel inclined as you move along.

For the journaling prompts, feel free to take a pen to the page or use a separate book, computer doc, or phone app to complete exercises that appeal or seem helpful to you. You can also speak your journal into a recorder, such as a phone's voice memo app, or discuss them aloud with a loved one or therapist. More than anything, we want you to make this book and its activities your own and use them in ways that most nourish you.

1

"Why Is This Happening to Me?"

AUGUST: IN HER OWN WORDS

My first panic attack struck on July 4, 2008. My partner, Mike, and I were newly married and driving from Los Angeles to Santa Barbara to stay with some of his longtime friends, who were a lot like family. He would work at an event, but for me, the trip was purely vacation. As a wedding gift, we were to stay in a special suite in a gorgeous ranch house. As we loaded ourselves and our travel bags into the SUV, I felt peaceful. Years of self-work had led me to my most self-accepting place yet. That all led to many rewards, from realizing my identity as a writer to meeting Mike, someone deeply kind, respectful, and genuine. Driving along, we chatted with ease between occasional shows of interest on NPR. Soon, postcard-like vistas of the Pacific Ocean appeared outside our windows. *So lucky . . .* I thought. But as we neared Santa Barbara, that "luck" turned into a nightmare. Terror struck me like a stranger yanking me from a car in a horror film. My heart thudded, my breathing grew heavy. *Was I sick?* Trembling and struggling to breathe, I noticed sweat dotting my chilled skin.

"Help!" I yelped.

Mike glanced at me from the driver's seat, concerned, then took the next exit and parked in a grocery store parking lot. He grasped my hand, his calm voice and lack of judgment like lifeboats I clung to.

"You're OK. . . ." He placed a warm hand on my forearm. "Take some slow breaths." As a medic, he had seen more than a few panic attacks and knew I was hyperventilating. Once my breathing had improved, we stepped out of the car. Walking around, my outward symptoms started to settle. On the inside, though, I felt paralyzed.

Mike bought us deli sandwiches and chilled drinks, aware that blood sugar levels can play a role in anxiety. While he didn't mention it at the time, I knew he was as perplexed as I was. Neither of us had seen me like this.

"Do you know why this is happening?" he asked gently, once we were situated back in the car.

I shook my head. "I feel like I can't . . . I don't know . . . like I'll die if we keep driving." Tears flooded my cheeks.

He paused. "Do you want to go home?"

"Yes!" My lungs welcomed oxygen. My shoulders eased.

We decided that I would be safest and calmest if he put me on a train back to L.A. And while he still says he felt terrible sending me off, I don't know that I have ever felt more loved. I started therapy soon after that event and another similar episode. As my therapist, a fortunate good fit, helped me skim through the layers of what might have led to the attacks, I admitted something I had been secretly struggling with. I had been longing for diet pills, stimulant concoctions I knew to be risky, even though I had zero desire to lose weight. Increasingly, those urges felt consuming. *Was I an addict?*

"What do you like about them?" she asked me.

"I feel like I need them. . . . They help my brain." The pills calmed me, even though I feared the adverse side effects, especially given that they weren't regulated or even legal to sell at pharmacies anymore.

The only way I could resist them was by consuming copious amounts of coffee and energy drinks, which occasionally put me into a groggy funk. And my ability to resist them or stick to reasonable amounts was dwindling.

Rather than suggest rehab, she asked me a series of questions, which led to an in-depth test that felt like analyzing my life's diary. Yes, I was hyper as a child and had an extremely low tolerance for boredom. Yes, I sometimes felt as though I couldn't rip myself away from something garnering my attention, and struggled profoundly to focus on other matters at will. Yes, a history of restless leg syndrome. Yes, losing things frequently. Yes, getting so lost in daydreams, I couldn't find my way out. Yes, yes, and yes . . .

Being diagnosed with ADHD was one of my most validating experiences, regardless of the fact that I've never been sure the words *attention deficit hyperactivity disorder* fully or accurately describe this type of neurodivergence. Having a name for it meant I could gain help, support, and understanding. After taking a prescribed stimulant medication, I took my first daytime nap in . . . perhaps ever. I felt like I'd donned glasses after years of squinting. I no longer felt either "stuck in the back of my brain" or bouncing around all over the place. My hyperfocus became manageable. I was still (neuro-atypical) me; I just didn't have to struggle so hard.

Around the same time, I learned that painful childhood wounds open wide for some people when they feel safest as adults, which is how I felt once Mike and I were married. That wound-opening makes sense, given that traumatic experiences shake one's sense of security. As children, in particular, we are supposed to feel safe and protected around adults.

Finally able to think straighter and having better understanding of the way my brain works, I felt myself healing, regardless of any lingering question marks. And for the next nearly eight years, I thrived more than ever. But then, everything shifted again.

By that point, we had moved to a more peaceful area of Los Angeles. I had started meditating for short spurts, something I hadn't before been capable of. And for the first time since puberty, I could read relatively well sitting still (versus, say, on the elliptical machine). Meditation can literally change brain chemistry, I'd read. *Had meditation cured my ADHD?* A meditation instructor I met seemed to think so. And while I questioned her suggestion that mental health medications render a person incapable of benefiting from meditation, I absorbed some of that stigma. So with my psychiatrist's permission, I stopped taking my pills.

Soon all of my symptoms returned, including the major depression that untreated ADHD led me to around adolescence, when hormonal changes joined my unbalanced brain. And as is typical with depression, activities I normally found pleasurable lost their sheen. Unable to think clearly enough to sort things out, I blamed other life stresses for my problems, barely noticing that when I went off the medication, I had stopped meditating too. I became stuck in a state of perpetual trauma and couldn't sort out why.

Sensing the need for support, I mentioned the "existential depression" I was developing to close friends. "I keep thinking about death," I confided in one friend, who replied, "Oh, that's just a writer thing! We're dark." Maybe she was right . . . ? "Look at everything you have to be grateful for," said another. *Indeed*, I concluded. *I should suck it up and be grateful*. Increasingly, though, I knew I was not OK. So

I went in for a physical, after getting so lost twice en route to that appointment that I missed it, where my doctor praised my shift from medication to meditation and suggested early perimenopause or a nutrient deficiency might be at play.

While all of this was happening, Mike had begun mountain climbing and trekking again, a longtime passion of his he had missed. He was growing increasingly involved in that community and related projects. I was, and remain, proud of him for these ventures. Yet when one of his trips came up suddenly amid a particularly dark period in my brain, I felt my lifeline leaving when I needed it most. I decided I would not let what I perceived as my own faults and struggles "get in his way."

So I gave him my blessing to take the trip, then spent the week he was away in debilitating terror and emotional pain. I barely slept, had to force myself to eat, and sobbed uncontrollably. I felt hyperalert, as though someone might attack me at any moment. I couldn't focus on *anything*, it seemed, besides my ruminating thoughts. So afraid of dying, I jotted down "I will not die today" in a notebook on my dresser, figuring what were the chances I would die after writing such a thing? And while I did eventually find a befitting therapist, a very bumpy road laid in between, even though I have the privilege of health insurance.

After Mike's return, most anything related to that trip could trigger my fight/flight/freeze reactions, nightmares, crying fits, and more. Making matters far worse, I fought and shunned myself for my feelings: *Why couldn't I just deal?* Certain I was ruining Mike's life and our relationship with my despair and inability to cope, the self-shaming became a trauma of its own, adding might and length to my trigger flares and putting strain on our relationship. In all, my mental health crisis would last the bulk of over a year.

Finally, in the wee hours of Christmas morning that year, amid another bout of nocturnal googling of my symptoms, it struck me that I might actually need my ADHD medication. After restarting it, my symptoms began lifting. But a few months later, seemingly out of the blue, I was triggered again. And then again. Bursts of dizzying paranoia, feeling unsafe, another panic attack. *Why?* It wasn't until watching *Leaving Neverland*, the HBO documentary centering on Wade Robson and James Safechuck, two survivors of abuse by Michael Jackson, that the remaining pieces clicked together. "My mind wouldn't go there," said one of the men in an Oprah Winfrey special about the film.

I sobbed as a fateful drive with my grandfather during childhood consumed my thoughts. We were on a road trip when he indicated that he and I would be sleeping together. While I didn't know what he meant, my excitement shifted to an ache that would linger long after an ice storm kept us from spending a night together. I was saved, I later thought—and I was, from so much. Even so, my world changed that day. And although I have long known that the experience impacted me, I never quite let my mind "go there" as far as the extent until recently. And the feeling I experienced when Mike was away on the trip that triggered me was exactly how I had felt in that car: I should have been safe, but safety left me. Meanwhile, unbeknownst to others, I was struggling mentally and emotionally leading up to that drive. And no one, not even I, understood why. But neither my brain nor my body ever forgot.

That epiphany made way for new layers of healing. My self-shaming shifted to self-compassion, and I felt able to take care of myself and seek out pleasure I now felt worthy of during my difficult days. And wouldn't you know: more pleasure brought more healing.

The morning after a cathartic therapy session, this book began formulating in my mind.

Soon after, while interviewing Jamila M. Dawson, a licensed marriage and family therapist (LMFT), for my podcast, I knew I wanted to seek her involvement. With her breadth of knowledge, based on both personal and professional experience, she articulates the intricacies of managing trauma in rare, needed, and approachable ways that I continue to learn from. Perhaps more so than ever, the world needs her pleasure-based, empathetic approach. I'm deeply grateful that she agreed to join me, and all of you, in this journey.

When my barrage of triggered episodes started a few years ago, I did what you may have done too: I searched (and searched, and searched) the web for answers. And that did help somewhat at times. But what we need throughout our deep self-work journeys can't be summarized in snappy headlines, articles, or listicles. Often, we leave with more questions than answers. Over time, I did find helpful modalities, studies, and research-based articles. I found supportive professionals to work with and learn from. And through a lot of trial, error, creativity, and support, I carved out a path that would bring me to where I am today: healthier in heart, mind, and soul. I want that same peaceful knowing for you, no matter where you are on your path, ideally with fewer bumps and roadblocks. Struggle is part of the journey, and full of potential gifts and lessons. I get that now. But I don't see a need to make things harder for ourselves than necessary.

So part of the answer to this first question, "Why is this happening?" is this: It's happening because you're human with a deeply feeling heart and a mind that wants to keep you safe. You've endured some really difficult stuff. You've been trying to cope as best you can.

That is admirable. And there is *absolutely nothing* wrong with you. As Jamila shared with me in that first podcast interview, trauma is a reasonable response to extraordinary events. You are not broken.

JAMILA: WHY SEX THERAPY?

People often ask me why I'm a sex therapist. I think they are confused because maybe they assume sex is simple, and so why would there need to be therapy for it? Other people seem titillated, perhaps thinking that I listen to salacious details of people's sex lives. Often, there is a sense from them that what I do is either dirty, beneath me (what kind of person are *you* that you talk about sex all the time?), or would inevitably become boring (how much can you actually *talk* about sex day after day; what is there to say?). And all of this simply confirms that there's *lots* of work to do.

My journey with trauma and pleasure-as-resilience is both personal and professional. I developed an expertise around it out of the need to survive my own trauma. But I teach about sexuality and relationships out of the desire to help build a society in which we can transcend trauma.

But why *sex* therapy?

Sex therapy is powerful and intimate and exhilarating work. In my private practice, clients come from a variety of backgrounds, ethnicities, sexual orientations, genders, gender presentations, relationship styles, and experiences. But I've come to see that each of them feels deeply unseen and unheard. Part of my work is to help see and listen to their hidden selves. As a therapist there is the power to protect, cultivate, influence, to discuss frightening ideas, to confront memories, put words to the unspeakable, and help people experience the reality that they are not alone and that they are here to create a life of vibrancy, pleasure, and connection.

Erotic feeling, which is our innate sense of aliveness, is one the most powerful forces on the planet. It fuels creativity, pleasure, and innovation. But when it is misunderstood, shamed, and forced to show up in a distorted form, it can also be used to harm, control, and damage others and the Self. Many of us have never known sexual expression/erotic expression as a positive force. Or maybe we have only glimpsed it but not known it or enjoyed it as an ongoing, generative way of life.

Too many of us have grown up living through trauma and finding ways to hide from its effects. Often this means attempts to escape, disconnect, punish, or control our bodies. I don't want people to be afraid or ashamed of themselves. I don't want people to put themselves, their emotions, their sensuality, or their capacity for feeling or for pleasure into a cage. I want people to learn to trust their bodies, for *you* to learn to trust *your* body; that your body wants you to survive and that ultimately we were made to thrive *in connection with* ourselves and others.

When I first began my private practice, I knew that traumatic experiences were prevalent. At the time, newly out of school, I thought I was prepared to help my clients "get better." In the clinical world, we often talk about symptom reduction as the focus of treatment. The goal is for people to no longer be bothered by insomnia, disordered eating, a chronic sense of unease, deep sadness, irritability, rage, fatigue, flashbacks, compulsive behaviors, passive or active suicidal ideation, and the host of other indicators of PTSD, depression, anxiety, or other "disorders." But as I worked with my clients to reduce their symptoms, making safety plans, listening to how they struggled to cope week after week, I could hear their shame, frustration, anger, exhaustion, despair, and, underneath all of that, the deep fear that they would always struggle with getting their bodies and minds to "act right" and "be normal." I saw that they feared that they would always feel alien in their own bodies; that their body was, and would remain, a site of distrust and that an iron grip of control over their lives was the best they could hope for.

It began to weigh on me that I was sitting with people's pain, but neither they nor I had a vision of what *could* be, something that went beyond mere survival. The absence of symptoms is not a *life*. My clients and I deserved better. We needed a paradigm that made room both for what is and for what can be.

It also took me a while to understand the fragility of the therapy room when measured against the larger culture. In this culture, we have been taught either to deny that our pain exists at all or that we can get rid of it through sheer willpower, positive thinking, or some other quick fix that's within our control. Although some elements in our lives can be shifted that way, in the aftermath of acute trauma or the continual onslaught of trauma-inducing circumstances that many of us live in, in the midst of a worldwide pandemic, the cold ghosts of trauma are not so easily exorcised. In the precious clinical hour that I have with my clients, we work to create space to grieve, to explore, to put words to the unspeakable, and to create new possibilities. But when my clients leave the office, those tender new understandings are swiftly buffeted by the harshness of so many aspects of life here in this world at this time in history.

Therapy is one type of change-work among others. It is simultaneously a particular kind of process and a particular kind of relationship, and at its best therapy concerns itself with the growth and healing of individuals and partners. And though this kind of change-work can be a profound experience for the clinician and their clients, the stark truth is that it is not enough or fast enough. We cannot forget that we are individuals within the larger group of humanity and that there is a critical immediacy to our societal and global challenges more so now than ever before. A somatic or mind/body-informed and trauma-informed approach needs to become foundational to how we engage with our partners, families, schools, businesses, and government. I've come to realize that I must expand my focus and help create larger cultural change so that there is a healthier world for my clients to reenter after our sessions.

With Pleasure is one more part of a larger movement to understand and reduce trauma while creating a foundation of pleasure and wellness for more people, including you. When August approached me to cowrite this with her, I was thrilled because here was a way to share and connect with others beyond my clinical practice. My hope in creating this book with August is to provide tools for individual support as well as to help push the culture further, one more rivulet in a stream that leads each of us to the knowledge that practices of pleasure can and will reshape our lives, contributing to many new and luscious futures.

Encouragement to Write

Writing is both real and metaphor. As you write you remake reality. Throughout this book, August and I offer you different opportunities to write your thoughts down. I can't stress enough the importance of writing or expressing your thoughts and feelings. There is something profoundly important and critical to one's healing process that stems from documenting your journey to create a record, an artifact of your experience and what you're realizing and learning along the way. I have heard from more than one client that the act of writing, or somehow putting words in written, visual, or aural form, can bring up feelings of fear and anxiety. So we will slowly work toward that, knowing that there are many ways to document your journey. It is one way of not escaping your process. Sometimes people don't want to write because they don't want to look at or hear those words. They don't want to feel those feelings. It's too much, and that's reasonable. And . . . I invite and gently challenge you to consider that the moments spent expressing your thoughts, having something that marks your journey and your courage, will be an incredible gift to yourself.

Grounding Exercise

With your hand over your heart, take several slow, deep breaths. Close your eyes, if it helps you relax and tune inward. Then, as you continue to breathe slowly, in and out, notice any tension you might be holding and do your best to release it. Mentally scan your body from your feet to your head, or from your head to your toes, noticing how each part of your body feels.

2

"What Is Happening to Me?"

THE BRAIN ON TRAUMA

Your brain is basically a whole world. Arguably the most precious and important organ in the human body, it controls and coordinates physical actions and reactions, allows you to think, learn, create, and express yourself, and experience virtually everything else that makes us human, from connecting with others and feeling aroused for sex or hungry for food to cultivating and storing memories.

As you may know, traumatic experiences can change the brain. When we first read or hear that, it can be easy to fear that we'll be forever altered—and not in a good way. You might stop at a headline claiming that very thing, fearful of what the contents might be. Thankfully, the negative shifts in your brain due to trauma, real as they are, do not have to be permanent. We can even experience love, joy, laughter, and, yes, *pleasure* throughout the healing process. Over time, we can become stronger and more resilient than ever.

When we realize that physiological changes take place during a trauma trigger flare, and that we do not choose or cause these changes, we may feel better able to ease up on ourselves, give ourselves grace to feel all of our emotions, and start chipping away at related shame. We can't force our brain chemistry to suddenly change any more than we can experience hunger or sleepiness on command, no matter who claims we can choose how we want to feel at any given moment, as though POOF! *Magical, instant contentment is just one little nudge away.* (Surely you've seen the memes.) In fact, attempting to presto-change-o trauma away is far more likely to cause harm than good. While understanding just what is happening in the brain is a huge first step in learning to manage trauma, it doesn't prevent us from getting triggered. We can set ourselves up for failure if we assume that cognitively understanding something will make the problem disappear.

THE SMOKE ALARM AND SECURITY SYSTEM

Two areas of the brain are affected when we feel triggered: the amygdala and the prefrontal cortex. Think of the amygdala as a sort of smoke alarm. The almond-shaped set of neurons detects threats in your environment ("smoke") and activates *fight, flight, freeze,* or *fawn* responses, so you can deal with the threat (hear the alert and put the fire out, flee, or stay planted), as part of your sympathetic nervous system. It also helps us store new emotional or threatening memories (so, among other things, we'll recall that fire and potentially prevent others).

The Fawn Response

The more recently identified fawn response involves attempting to avoid conflict and additional trauma by appeasing others. Some of the ways it might play out include helping or supporting someone who seems threatening, feeling unable to say no when you wish to, or feeling responsible for other people's harmful actions. From a sex and relationship standpoint, fawning might show up as abandoning your desires or needs in order to please a partner or assuming blame when someone you're dating gets upset or crosses your boundaries.

The prefrontal cortex is more like a security system in your house or apartment building. Situated just behind your forehead, this part of the brain regulates your awareness and attention (panning around for potential threats, in the case of life after trauma). It also allows us to make decisions, initiates voluntary behavior, determines the significance of events, regulates our emotions, and corrects or inhibits dysfunctional reactions.

When the brain senses a threat, the fight, flight, freeze, or fawn response releases a few chemicals: glucose, adrenaline, and norepinephrine. If this carries on, the brain prompts your pituitary gland and hypothalamus to release the stress hormone cortisol. Meanwhile, your prefrontal cortex assesses the threat and either calms or revs up your fight/flight/freeze/fawn reaction.

When we're experiencing residual effects of trauma, we can have a hyperreactive amygdala and an underactivated prefrontal cortex. This is a bit like having a smoke alarm that goes off at the slightest hint of a fire, such as from steam during a hot shower or when you're boiling water on a stove. And rather than calm the reaction down, which would happen in someone who isn't dealing with trauma complications, the monitoring system sort of looks the other way.

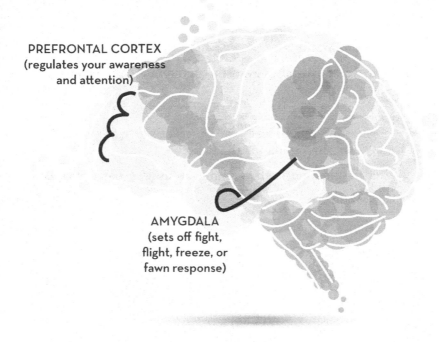

PREFRONTAL CORTEX
(regulates your awareness
and attention)

AMYGDALA
(sets off fight,
flight, freeze, or
fawn response)

All of this can lead to or heighten trauma responses:

- Appetite changes
- Avoidance of people, places trauma-related
- Depersonalization, or feeling as though you're detached from your body
- Derealization, or feeling as though "things aren't real"
- Difficulty experiencing or prioritizing pleasure
- Dissociation, or disconnecting from your thoughts, feelings, memories, or sense of identity
- Emotional distress after exposure to traumatic reminders
- Feeling isolated or as though no one could understand you
- Fight, flight, freeze, or fawn responses

- Flashbacks
- Inability to recall key aspects of the trauma
- Irritability or aggression
- Negative self-talk
- Physical reactivity after exposure to traumatic reminders
- Reduced self-esteem
- Risky or destructive behavior
- Ruminating on trauma-related thoughts
- Sexual dysfunction, such as fearing arousal, sexual avoidance
- Sleep problems
- Upsetting memories
- Nightmares

When we're reminded of a traumatic event from the past, the brain can perceive it as a threat that is just as harmful as the original event. The brain can't tell the difference between a true threat and a perceived one, potentially making the perceived one equally problematic. Just because a threat is "perceived," versus happening in real life, doesn't make it any less worthy of addressing. A trauma response, or being triggered or activated, is the body's way of protecting itself from perceived danger. It immediately bypasses the part of our brain responsible for rational decisions. This can be a profoundly frustrating idea to sit with when we just want to get rid of feeling bad or are living in fear, awaiting the next "attack."

When we've had a traumatic experience or live within traumatizing circumstances, it can feel as though at any moment we could get a trauma flare, when the present drops away into an abyss and we are lost in that place, unable to understand what is happening, not able to get out, and shaken in our core when we finally emerge. Often there is a secondary experience of shame or anger that this "thing" has taken us over and we were helpless. In our shame, bewilderment, or anger, we may act in ways that hurt or confuse ourselves or others.

A far more helpful aim? To learn to flow with and move through trauma flares in healthful, embodied ways. And to know that pleasure is there for us in any given moment, to enhance our lives and abilities to navigate trauma in ways that bolster, rather than dim, us. As we heighten our understanding about ways trauma and pleasure impact the brain and body, we can better leverage these responses for deeper awareness and fuller lives.

> Pleasure: a feeling of happiness, enjoyment, or satisfaction; a pleasant or pleasing feeling; an activity that is done for enjoyment; something or someone that causes a feeling of happiness, enjoyment, or satisfaction

THE BRAIN ON PLEASURE

Typically when we hear or read about the brain and pleasure, the context is pretty negative. A quick web search of the topic draws up headlines like "How Addiction Hijacks the Brain," and articles that define "pleasure" as "the good feeling you get in response to drugs." Indeed, addiction is an important and worthy topic. It's also not the only subject that matters in terms of neuroscience and pleasure. Not remotely. True pleasure isn't about a rapid high, quick "fix," or pathology. It's an authentic goodness we are built to experience and embrace.

From a physiological perspective, pleasurable feelings stem from the release of chemical messengers, especially dopamine, in the brain's reward center. Dopamine is a bit like your supportive best friend, the person who lets you know when to expect something positive: *Your birthday party is going to be lit!* Also like a trusted friend, dopamine drives us to seek that which feels rewarding: *If it makes your heart sing, GO FOR IT. You are worthy.*

If only the brain naturally prompted feelings of self-worthiness, along with those chemicals . . . Given the many factors that can stand in the way, such as trauma, other emotional wounds, systemic oppression, and societal messaging, getting to that place often takes time, intention, and practice. Mighty as the brain is, it is not immune to difficulty. When we are triggered, it's natural and common to feel more focused on surviving, heartache, or fear. Allowing for those feelings, practicing self-care, and prioritizing pleasure can help ease those heavy burdens.

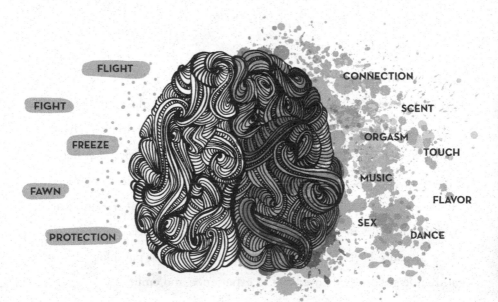

DIGGING DEEPER INTO PLEASURE

We all experience pleasure uniquely, based on factors such as lived experience, genetics, and upbringing. Creating or listening to music, dancing (yes, even if you're not "good" at it), and savoring art may come close to stimulating the brain's reward center powerfully, and not only elevate pleasurable feelings, but also help manage symptoms of PTSD. From a sex standpoint, orgasm and ejaculation have been linked with improved blood flow to the cerebellum, the brain area that helps us process emotions. For folks who are inclined, pleasurable sex and orgasm can also help minimize stress and anxiety, while instilling a sense of bliss or peacefulness. Almost anything that engages one or more of our senses—taste, touch, smell, hearing, sight—in positive ways can invite the myriad perks of pleasure.

When you read all of that, you might think, "Sure, that makes sense. Pleasure makes us feel good." It can seem like a no-brainer. Fortunately and unfortunately, the implementation isn't so simple. As adrienne maree brown asserts in her 2019 book, *Pleasure Activism: The Politics of Feeling Good*, "Our imaginations—particularly the parts of our imaginations that hold what we most desire, what brings us pleasure, what makes us scream yes—are where we must seed the future, turn toward justice and liberation, and reprogram ourselves to desire sexually and erotically empowered lives." Here's the unfortunate part: barriers stand in the way for many of us, such as racist systems, misogyny, consumerism, productivity culture, religious messaging, caregiver burnout—and the list goes on. Thankfully, we can do our best to work around or through these barriers if we commit to doing so. This work starts with examining our relationship with pleasure.

Jot down a list of activities that bring you pleasure. What do you notice about these practices? Is it easy or difficult to think of these activities?

DESIREE: TRUST, DISABILITY, AND BDSM

Desiree was molested as a child. During her early adulthood, she survived an abusive relationship with a man who only wanted to get her pregnant. As a result, she lives with fear of strangers' touch. "If they put a hand on my shoulder without telling me, it scares me," she said. "There are times when I go to a doctor or physical therapist and having someone touch me or see me naked, makes me feel scared and paralyzed. I stay quiet. I just hope it's over soon."

Desiree said that "lots and lots of therapy" has helped her hugely, as has plentiful inner work and learning to be kind to herself while understanding that she can't control everything or attain perfection. "I still beat myself up mentally, but now I have coping skills to take care of myself when I am triggered or anxious," she shared. "I cope by journaling, reading, or talking to my friends or therapist. I used to keep everything to myself."

From a sexuality standpoint, she has found healing through BDSM, which she compared to a personal form of meditation. "I rarely have moments in which my mind stops," she said of her experiences with other types of sex. "Without BDSM, I usually start thinking about what I'm doing wrong, if I'm safe or if I even deserve pleasure. I'm very insecure and easily startled, so it's important for me to get out of my head and trust my partner."

Desiree isn't alone in experiencing these benefits. Numerous studies and anecdotal data show that BDSM—or erotic practices involving bondage and discipline, dominance and submission, and/or sadism and masochism—can bring healing to people who've endured trauma. (It's important to note that plenty of people are drawn to BDSM for other valid reasons too.) Research conducted at Widener University concluded that "achieving subspace during consensual BDSM interactions might result in a reduction of physical and emotional stress in the submissive partner, as well as heightened intimacy between participants." Practicing BDSM helps some folks create more conscientiousness, feel less rejection-sensitive, or enjoy role-playing scenes in which a previously traumatic occurrence is reenacted in a safe setting where you decide the outcome.

Desiree said she didn't have sex until age twenty-four, after she had finished college. Before then, her father didn't want her to move out because she's paralyzed and uses a wheelchair, factors that aren't often the easiest to navigate in an ableist culture. During college, her self-confidence flourished and she started flirting, with the sense that she knew what she was doing. Paired with the privacy she had longed for, she finally felt comfortable and assured exploring her sexuality as a disabled woman. Although Desiree's first boyfriend was abusive, she learned important lessons about her body and pleasure before the relationship ended, which came as a surprise. At the time, she didn't think she was capable of experiencing orgasm. Then one day, when they were both tipsy and engaged in rough sex, she felt a surge of orgasmic bliss. "He was dominant and I was passive," she noted. "I don't know what he did or if the alcohol made me get out of my head, but I felt an out-of-body experience and I noticed that my clit was out and erect, just like a little penis! It was amazing and I was surprised by my own body."

Desiree's growth and healing from trauma have revealed themselves in numerous ways, more so in recent years. After dating people she described as aggressive and emotionally unavailable, she found herself drawn to a gentle, caring man last year. To him, she said, she opened her whole heart. While that relationship didn't last, she considers it the best she has ever experienced. Within it, she felt safe and secure. "He even noticed that my confidence increased after we started dating," she added. "I learned to trust more. . . . I finally knew what it felt like when someone loved you back."

Currently single, Desiree said she hopes to find another caring person to explore sensual pleasure with. Systems of ableism and misogyny continue to fuel her distrust in men, making things difficult in certain ways, but she sincerely believes in love. "I have made the most of my sex life by believing in myself," she said. "When I'm in bed, guys seem to forget that I'm paralyzed and that helps me feel better. Sometimes I forget about my disability and trauma. I just try to have fun."

> The erotic is a measure between the beginnings of our sense of self and the chaos of our strongest feelings. It is an internal sense of satisfaction to which, once we have experienced it, we know we can aspire. For having experienced the fullness of this depth of feeling and recognizing its power, in honour and self-respect we can require no less of ourselves.
> —Audre Lorde, *Uses of the Erotic: The Erotic as Power*

Jamila's Reflections

Many of Desiree's experiences are shared by clients I've seen over the years. Some of the patterns include her fear and silent endurance during her doctor's appointments. Even when we rationally know that we are going into a space that should be safe, feelings of intense vulnerability, fear, anger, and other unpleasant emotions can rise up. We may feel trapped between our need to take care of ourselves by going to our doctor's appointments and our body's heightened sense of uncertainty, disgust, or alarm at the prospect of being in the situation.

When that happens, we may engage in a variety of behaviors to move away from the discomfort that medical/physical appointments engender. Sometimes people knowingly choose not to make health care appointments because doing so is simply too overwhelming, or they may make an appointment but completely forget about it on the day of. Others experience headaches or stomachaches leading up to such appointments. If they are able to attend the appointment, some people become so dysregulated afterward that driving can become dangerous and using public transportation, disorienting. Moods can take a severe dip. Tears, anger, intense sadness, irritability, not eating or eating too much that day are all possible outcomes of an emotionally stressed nervous system. They may get in a fight with a loved one or withdraw from them. When clients report these experiences, I strongly encourage them to try to place these responses in a "container of gentleness." They are not "weak," "acting like a child," or "being ridiculous." On the contrary, the body is speaking its distress the only way it knows how, by loudly signaling that something *feels* wrong and that there is a threat to our perceived/actual sense of safety.

If we practice moving toward our body's distress, however—meaning noticing our body's reactions, taking them seriously, and working *with* our body, not against it—we give ourselves a better chance of mitigating or reducing distress or harm to ourselves or those who love us.

KM: FINDING ZEN

KM Huber's trauma stems from what she considers a two-pronged event centered around her mother. "My family bond was with an aunt and uncle who cared for me for the first five years of my life," she recalled. "My parents worked and I lived with them, but in this extended family situation, I fell in love with my Aunt Mary and adopted the rather foul mouth of my Uncle Mick."

When she started school, her mother stopped working outside of the home and her sister, Debbie, was born. Together, they "tried to be a family," and her father put in for a job transfer to another state, a distance away he seemed to deem necessary. "I didn't know how much I didn't like my mother until we were without her family around," KM said. "In North Dakota, we were around my father's family somewhat but not as close. This is when I remember lying a lot; I hadn't lost my uncle's swagger. I wasn't a pleasant child; I missed my Aunt Mary a lot."

Four months before KM's tenth birthday, four-year-old Debbie was killed in a freak car accident, some of which KM witnessed. Once it happened, she called out Debbie's name. A neighbor alerted their dad, who came running and swooped Debbie up in his arms. When he handed her to KM's mom, the woman looked at KM and said, "Why didn't you watch her?"

"That would be a trigger for me, especially later years into adulthood," KM said of that comment. "I could blame my mother, and I did, but the bigger issue was believing I didn't deserve to live. Debbie had lost her life because of me, so how could anything I ever did be of worth? It would take me until my late fifties to understand that was my albatross."

More than anything else from the day of the accident, KM recalls watching her parents drive away in her father's fire engine–red 1957 Chevy Bel Air, her mother holding Debbie in the back seat. They didn't speed away, perhaps knowing there was little to be done. KM stood there watching for some time, her eyes locked on where the car had been, her young mind unable to grasp what was fully happening. "I remember [thinking] . . . something like, *that does it* or *that's it*," she said. "I knew it was the final break with my family."

Over thirty years later, KM went to see a psychiatrist—not to discuss Debbie's death, but to learn to deal with her then-partner's children. By then, she seemed to have traded perpetual lying with drinking. "I drank a lot and lived as if I were waiting for someone or something to stop me but always, I remained detached," she added. "Of course, this is retrospective thinking, but I think that's exactly what happened."

Nearly two decades later, as she approached her late fifties, her "whole world shattered" when she said she lost her health, her home, and, by way of a medical retirement, her job. She'd been experiencing increasingly debilitating symptoms, which she had been told twenty years prior derived from multiple sclerosis. In reality, she had been struggling with Sjogren's syndrome, rheumatoid arthritis, and degenerative disc disease.

"All these years had taken quite a toll on my health and finally my body said stop or 'That's it!,' as my mother was so fond of saying," KM noted. "So, I found myself in the living room of my two-story condo with a diabetic, aging beagle, boxes of books all around us. As always, I turned to writing, but it couldn't be writing as it had always been. I didn't even try that. And I found myself trying to write about my sister's death, but I couldn't."

Therein blossomed her epiphany: she couldn't continue living as she had been, and many of her trials stemmed from her childhood traumas. "That's when I knew all of my life up to that moment had been tied to two things," she said, "leaving my Aunt Mary and watching my sister die." Especially back then, she said, people were expected to "stuff" their emotions. And for decades, that's what she did. "I lived a life I rarely liked and so often escaped through sex, detached, just purely for the physical feeling, and through alcohol," she said, adding that she frequently sought sex with the "wrong people," including married men, though she identifies as lesbian.

Thanks to those realizations and years of compassionate self-work, KM's life is far different now: more authentic, richer, and full of creativity. It's a life she not only likes, but cherishes. More than anything, she credits Zen practice, including mindfulness, meditation, and "staying open to life as it is," for her most powerful growth. All of that started when she came upon meditation sessions online. At the time, KM felt desperate for alternatives to traditional medicine that she felt had failed her.

"During one of these sessions, there was a guided meditation in which I was once again a nine-year-old girl with my three-year-old sister, Debbie, and we took each other's hands and walked away together," she recalled. "It is and has been the most powerful meditative moment of my life. She and I were only children. It was an accident. There was no fault, no blame." She extended her meditation practice to thirty minutes a day, then came upon a webinar led by Pema Chödrön, which brought "another life-changing moment." Thirty minutes a day became an hour a day and she shifted from closed-eye transcendental meditation to mindfulness meditation, staying aware of her surroundings. She read Chödrön's *How to Meditate* and then her iconic *When Things Fall Apart*.

"I don't know how many times I have read [*When Things Fall Apart*] and will read it, but it's the one book I would have with me on a deserted island," she said. "I can't help but think it's ironic that Zen, the insistence on being here, right now, regardless, is what has helped me make the shift from my sister's death and all of that abusive behavior to acceptance and self-compassion."

Jamila's Reflections

One element that strikes me about KM's story is that healing really can happen at any age. The United States is absolutely a youth-obsessed culture. We have so many "under thirty" or "under forty" lists, and there is this deep preoccupation with the idea that if it doesn't happen when we're young, then it will never happen and we should just give up or we didn't try hard enough. What KM's story illuminates is that change and growth and healing and a deep sense of vibrancy in one's life can happen at any point along the life span, and that those subsequent years can be filled with a richness and a contentment that we did not know could exist. And so it's important to continue to hold out possibility for our growth and for the growth of other people.

There is something so haunting and profoundly sad about the image of a little girl watching her family drive away and knowing in her body that something is over and that her life is forever changed. Children are acutely and wonderfully attuned to feeling and experiencing life. In some ways, they are pure emotion. And this capacity is one of the reasons why watching children grow and interacting with children are such amazing balms to the soul. So inspiring, they can bring deep joy. The cost of this is that children can deeply internalize a sense of responsibility and feel experiences so profoundly that in some ways they become lodged in the body. In response to trauma, the psyche contorts around that emotional fragmenting and obstructs the child's development. When KM was finally forced to confront her pain, her trauma, her loss, and the years of disconnection and begin to practice being in the present moment, she had newfound space to recognize what she needed to grieve and to choose the life she wanted to live.

Grounding Exercise

Notice shades of a color. Look around the room or area you're in and notice one color. Then scan your surroundings, looking for every instance and shade of that color you can find. Describe them aloud, if you wish. Maybe you see egg yolk–yellow, pale yellow, and yellow with hints of orange. If you're blind, choose another sense. Touch and name all of the textures you can find around you, for example, or move your attention to every sound you can hear, near or far.

3

"How Can I Stop This?"

Here's a difficult truth that can take some time and effort to wrap our heads around. When we've been activated, our job is not to try to stop triggers from ever cropping up again, or to somehow "fix" ourselves so we won't experience negative effects ever again. As we mentioned earlier, these types of assumptions can set us up to fail. Our primary responsibility is to love ourselves through it as best we can.

Yes, we know. "Just love yourself!" might sound a bit hokey. In this case, however, there is no "just" about it. And we aren't talking about attempting to flip a mental switch or adopt a new "attitude" by prompting magical, adoring self-talk, as you might have heard an Instagrammer suggest. Oxford Languages dictionaries define self-love as a "regard for one's own well-being and happiness; chiefly considered as a desirable rather than narcissistic characteristic." Such definitions get self-love somewhat wrong in an important way, by limiting the term to a noun. By its truest definition, self-love is an action, a verb, a commitment, and a practice. It is mighty. It can be difficult. And it is always, always worthwhile.

When we attempt to bully ourselves into stopping activated flares, we do the *opposite* of self-love while working against its existence. It's a bit like working long hours and skimping on sleep and fluids when you have the flu. Or working yourself harder than usual because you're certain the virus is entirely your fault. Without sufficient rest and hydration, and with the added stress of self-shaming, your symptoms can worsen and lead to potentially serious complications. The antidote, at least in part, is practicing authentic self-love. Every step toward this end counts, especially during the most challenging of times.

ANNE: RECLAIMING SELF-WORTH

Anne was in an abusive relationship with a man she described as "somewhere on the narcissist/sociopath spectrum" for thirty-one years. They met when she was just thirteen. "Over time, he made me believe I was very broken sexually and in most every way," she said. "I learned to disconnect from him and from sex and even from my own body in order to orgasm." Orgasm was a frequent requirement in the relationship, whether she felt inclined or not, she added, because he considered her climaxes signs of his vigor and skill. Meanwhile, he shamed her any time she indicated her own sexual desire; it had to be his choice, not hers.

Gradually, she reached a turning point. "I finally decided I deserved better or that there could be more," she recalled. Finding her own physical strength through lifting weights helped provide her with the confidence to leave. She wasn't dieting or engaging in White supremacy–fueled fat phobia, as so many of us fall prey to in an attempt to better ourselves. Rather, she connected with her body and mind's inherent capability that she had been distanced from for too long.

"People would say, 'Draw from your pain or your anger,'" she shared. "I didn't really get that from [weight lifting]. . . . I didn't know I was strong. I had never been strong at anything or good at anything or capable at anything my whole life." Growing up, Anne's parents and siblings struggled with extensive drug, alcohol, and mental health issues. In an effort to compensate for or avoid adding to familial problems, she attended church faithfully, "following every rule." She got straight As in school. And then, when she met and believed she was in love with a boy at age thirteen, she believed he would save her. Instead, she found herself entrenched in his behaviors of manipulation and control.

So when Anne began to excel at weight training, so much so that she landed regional records, she had a hard time wrapping her brain around her success. Little by little, though, she embraced the increasing strength of her body as signs that she was powerful and worthy of a better life. Accolades are nice, she believes, but her real prize has been the true self-love she has cultivated and the freedom she has found from the sources of her traumas. Early in her healing process, she started to realize that her sexuality could shift as well. "About three years before my marriage ended, I started kind of pulling away from religion, so I started wanting to learn my body. I realized masturbation was OK. I started realizing that pleasure was OK. At that point, I just made the choice I'm going to have a good sex life, whether I'm married to someone crappy or not. Like I can make that happen for me."

At that point, Anne started studying sexuality and learning about her anatomy, her capacity for pleasure, and "how linked the body is to the brain." In doing so, she realized that neither she nor her body were broken. Once she entered a new, far healthier intimate relationship with a new partner, she started to grieve all she had lost by not getting to those conclusions sooner—a process that was painful, but also important for her healing. Counseling and continued self-work have brought her to a place where she practices grace and compassion with herself, as well as gratitude for all she has learned, both because of and in spite of her darkest times. She credits all of this to leading her to a place where she's happier than ever, not because she's smiling all the time, as she used to feel pressured to do, but because she can live as her whole, authentic self.

"There's safety when you can show all of yourself and be completely open and still be accepted," she said. "And if you do that, you will find people who accept you, rather than feel the need to change yourself to be who they need you to be or to make them comfortable."

In what ways can you actively care for yourself today or on a daily basis? What simple tools or practices can you keep in mind for caring for yourself when you feel activated?

TRIGGERED DURING SEX: HELPFUL PRACTICES

We can't often predict precisely when we'll feel triggered. But it can happen when we are feeling particularly relaxed, particularly stimulated/excited, or we are experiencing a new level of care or safety. This is why triggers can happen during our sexual encounters. It may seem counterintuitive, but in the aforementioned states, we are sometimes more aware of our bodies and so our bodies can read and relay signals more easily than when we are distracted. When we're activated during sex, it's not uncommon to feel unsure about the best steps to take. One of the first helpful steps you can take is knowing or reminding yourself that such flare-ups are not a sign of weakness. They are an opportunity for you and your partner(s) to tend to your needs. Slowing down or pausing, utilizing a grounding exercise, and processing what you experienced with a loved one, therapist, or through journaling or other means of self-reflection once you're no longer in an activated state can help tremendously. Keep in mind that you don't have to reveal everything you're going through and why as it's happening. (In many cases, that's not even possible.) Instead, simply request a break. Or use a predetermined safe word, such as "yellow" for "I need to slow down" or "red" for "stop."

Because trauma reactions interfere with executive function, recalling what steps to take in the moment can be challenging. If you're concerned that that may happen, consider keeping the following list, or items that especially strike you, nearby. Keep this book in your bedroom, for example, or take a photo of the list to keep on your phone. These grounding exercises can help by replacing that which felt triggering with calmness or relaxation. Take as long as you need with whatever practices you choose.

- Take slow, deep breaths, if you're able. You could lead the breathing between you and a partner. Or, if needed or it feels helpful, a partner can lead the breathing and you can follow their breathing pattern.

- Squeeze your muscles as you do a mental scan of your body, from head to toe, doing your best to release any tension you notice.

- Wrap your arms around yourself and firmly hug your body. Close your eyes, if you wish, and really take the sensations and act of self-care in.

- Catch a lover's gaze with your own. It can feel intimately soothing and melt away feelings of isolation that can crop up during activation. In other cases, eye contact may feel too intense.

Choose the option that feels most comforting, knowing that you can stop (or start) any of these practices at any time.

- Stop the sex and/or move to another position or activity. Or continue in a different room or room area, if that feels comforting.
- Cuddle or just lay side by side. Do so as long as you desire.
- Place your hand on your heart or your partner's heart. Observe the heartbeat.
- Apply a cool or warm towel to your skin. Keep one by the bed for such uses, if possible.

Jamila's Reflections

Like so many other people's stories, Anne's experiences of abuse separated her sexual response and her sexuality from her own bodily sovereignty. Even her orgasms were not hers to enjoy as an expression of her pleasure, but only as proof of her husband's skill. When our sexuality, sexual pleasure, and vitality are co-opted over a long period of time, we may not have access to anything we can recognize as anger or even pain. Anne's story speaks to why it is not always helpful to assume that channeling our emotions can be helpful; sometimes because of the deep harm done, we simply cannot find them. Her path back to her body was feeling her body's capacity for strength and capacity for change. And when the body is aware, that is a wonderful foundation for psychological change.

Script for Talking About Triggers

I know that often we may feel afraid or ashamed to say

something to our sex partners for fear of alienating them or hurting them. But a caring partner wants to know if you're in distress and wants to help. If we ignore our body's signals that we are activated, we train ourselves to override our body's sense of safety, and that can prevent us from experiencing reparative moments in real time.

One of the implicit cultural messages we get is that once sex starts, it has to continue "to the end." This is not true. A sexual encounter can and should stop for any reason at any time. Great sex is not a train you get on as a passive passenger and wait to "get off" at your stop. It is a place, an idyll where you can relax, explore, pause, savor, run around, or leave altogether when you choose. It's important to communicate if we need to "leave," but again, you and your partner(s) are not stuck and you can return there at any time. If you and/or a partner end a sexual encounter, you can pick back up when you're able. If you ever need to take a break for any reason, such as you or they have a cramp, need to go to the bathroom, feel thirsty or hungry, or desire an emotional pause, that need is sufficient and legitimate. This practice allows the body to learn that relief and pleasure are accessible at any time. Finding the words in the moment is sometimes a monumental struggle, so here is a script you can use in the immediate moment of being activated:

Hey, something is wrong/I'm not OK right now/something is happening.

I need some silence.

I need to be cuddled.

I need you to lightly hold my hand.

I need to cry.

Here is a script if you want to initiate a conversation with a sex or intimate partner when you feel more back in your body:

I am working to understand myself and my past and so I am seeing a therapist/read a book/article about trauma, and it really made a lot of sense to me about how and why I sometimes act the way I do. I would really like your help in . . . Here are some things that I would like to ask of you/ways that you can help me . . .

Then list three specific requests.

1. _____
2. _____
3. _____

For Partners

As the partner of someone who has or is experiencing trauma, you may find it confusing, or even scary, to not know what is happening internally for your partner or to know what's happening and yet feel helpless to protect them from being activated. It's critical to know that you are not responsible for what they endured or continue to endure. But there are absolutely concrete steps that you can take, both in the moment and later on, to support them and sustain yourself.

If you are paying attention to your partner's verbal

and physical expressions, you may be able to tell when they aren't completely present, but sometimes you can't. Both are OK. What matters most are understanding their boundaries, creating your own boundaries, providing gentle check-ins, not personalizing their body's reactions, and creating shared understandings of what to do when a trauma flare happens.

Here is a script for possible things to say in a gentle tone in the moment. Simple words and short questions can be very helpful:

Hey, are you here with me?

You seem far away right now; how can I help?

What do you need right now?

Here is a script for developing a shared plan of ongoing support. Both of your needs may change over time, so it's important to revisit this conversation:

I am working to understand how trauma affects you and us. I am seeing a therapist/read a book/article about trauma, and it's helpful to know that we don't have to figure this out alone. I would really like your help in . . . Here are some things that I would like to ask of you . . . Here are ways that you can help me to support you better . . . Then list three specific requests or questions.

1._____

2._____

3._____

WOLF: CHOSEN FAMILY, CONSENT, AND CIS MALE SURVIVORS

For as long as he can remember, Wolf knew that the harm he endured throughout his childhood was abuse. "I always knew what was going on was wrong," he said, of his father's physical and emotional abuse. Sexual abuse by a neighbor before he reached kindergarten and being raped by two teenage girls for seven hours a few years later added to and exacerbated the ongoing trauma. "I never was a person that normalized it. I luckily learned the opposite lesson, so I was very good about not continuing the cycle or keeping the cycle up. But I did have a lot of very, very negative defense mechanisms that I used to protect myself and shield myself."

When Wolf turned twelve, his parents stopped allowing him to come home if he was out late into the night. Rather than creating boundaries to enforce healthy behavior and safety, his parents set this rule to protect their own sleep. He said that these restrictions, while harsh and uncaring, gave him a lot of welcomed freedom. He used it to avoid being around his dad as much as possible, spending time at an underage club until they closed and then roaming the Alaska streets, where he felt far safer than he felt at home.

At one point during his teens, after a blowup argument, Wolf tried to stand up for himself. When he did, his father threatened to beat him to death. Once things seemed to have calmed down for the time being, Wolf went to the backyard to let his frustration out by kicking a tree, not realizing that his dad witnessed his typically private ritual. His dad told Wolf's best friend that if he didn't get him out of the house, Wolf would try to kill him. That fall, Wolf, who had tested out of high school during his tenth-grade year, was sent to Job Corps for vocational training. There, he spoke openly for the first time to adults, including counselors, about the abuse he had endured. Prior to that, he had only confided in his friends when they were drunk or stoned, so there was little chance they'd remember. "I kind of acted more like a kid there than I pretty much did most of my life," he recalled about his time at Job Corps. "You know, having the whole cliquey high school experience and that whole thing and going to the mall with my friends. I felt I was able to fall out of survival mode."

Over the years, Wolf spent a great deal of time wondering how his father could say, "I love you, I'll protect you, I'll never let anyone hurt you," and then put his head through a wall. He studied psychology, philosophy, and sociology, as well as every religious manual he could get his hands on. "I deep-dived into psychology and Maslow and all of that stuff to try to figure out an answer," he added. "And I never truly found out. I got a lot of understanding about where abuse cycles come from . . . but in the end, my dad was just an asshole."

The collective trauma has caused a range of challenges around sex. He finds physical traits in women that mirror his abuser's appearance triggering, which makes it very difficult for him to connect with such women intimately. And because the rape that his abuser took part in involved hours of intentional humiliation, he struggles with sex in general, especially if it lasts more than a brief amount of time. It's not that he isn't interested in sex, he noted, but that harmful people led him to feel extremely uncomfortable with elements of it. "I have a lot of body and image issues and shame and consciousness toward certain aspects of my body as a result of that that have just never resolved," he said. "And that's some of the stuff I know I need to speak to a therapist about . . . but when you're poor, you can't afford it."

Wolf relies heavily on his chosen family, consisting of a network of friends, most of whom have dealt with similar trauma, for community and support—much of which comes by way of him helping others, "probably to a fault." He spends time listening to fellow survivors, lending an empathetic ear, and helping when he can. In doing so, he's found that one reaction many survivors have regarding sex is feeling deeply rejected when a partner isn't up for it. "Any time you feel or see something as a slight or a disregard or dismissal, it impacts you super heavily, to where most of the time if your partner would be like, 'Oh, I'm not horny right now,' it feels like, 'You're not worthy. You're not wanted. You're not needed.' It hits you harder. And I believe that comes from that trauma place of humiliation." For these reasons, Wolf believes that trauma survivors, in particular, need thorough education about consent, both to help ease those emotional burdens and to guard against unintentionally hurting someone by violating their boundaries, "without any maliciousness, but based on your own traumas."

Wolf has learned a great deal about consent, communication, boundaries, and sex through BDSM. While he knows that trauma doesn't automatically lead a person to interest in BDSM, that it isn't a prerequisite, he's also found that every person he's connected with in the community has endured trauma and finds the practices healing. "There's a language that we speak with each other that kind of talks about that without really speaking, where you're talking about safety and trust, and you're speaking about your trauma," he said. "You're speaking about your pain and you're speaking about what you've been through, but you're not actually talking about it. So that helped me a lot as well."

More societal awareness and support around sexual assault toward

men would have helped Wolf too. He wishes more people understand that boys, men, and anyone with a penis can be victimized,
just as much as women, femmes, and folks with vulvas; it's just less
talked about, which can worsen the impact of the trauma and too
often stands in a person's way of getting needed care. "My first sexual trauma experience was with women and my last sexual trauma
experience was with women," he said. "And being a cis male that's
been through sexual trauma and then having that on top of it, it's
not something that's recognized or talked about. It wasn't until 2014
that envelopment was even considered sexual assault. So that is very
important for me to speak about."

Jamila's Reflections

One of the heartbreaking parts of Wolf's story is his isolation, given
how society creates false narratives about gender. Unfortunately, we
continue to see that boys, men, and those with penises are too often
ridiculed or ignored when it comes to sexual, emotional, and psychological abuse. Abusive behaviors harm everybody. Patriarchy harms
everybody. White supremacy harms everybody. Ignoring the needs
of children harms everybody. Simply because somebody is a cis man
does not mean that they are not a victim or survivor of abuse. The
experience of abuse harms and changes every person it happens to,
and we need to cultivate a culture in which people of all genders are
protected and cared for, and in which, if someone is harmed, they
have access to care. For some of my clients who are cis men who have
experienced emotional, sexual, or psychological abuse, a huge part
of their trauma comes from shame. They have come to experience no
one believing them or people minimizing their experience and chalking

it up to "Oh, I guess you were turned into a man early" or "Aren't you lucky that that happened so quickly? What a lady-killer." All of these statements invalidate the survivor's story and perpetuate harmful stereotypes around what's expected of men and folks of all genders. If a person does not consent or changes their consent and no longer wants to engage in an activity, *it makes no difference what their gender is.* Their consent is being violated if the activity continues. Wolf's experience demonstrates how we, as a culture, have certain expectations for men and varied expectations for others. This poses danger for all of us.

As survivors, it's important to realize that if someone violates our consent, we do not have to justify or rationalize our desire to find help. Nor do we need to attempt to continue activities that feel violating or as though they're moving in a risky direction because we feel we "should" consider them acceptable or pleasurable. If certain words or behaviors feel triggering, even if they seem benign on the surface, you do not need to attempt to bear them in silence or attempt to justify why they feel risky or harmful. You don't need to make excuses or explain yourself. You deserve safety and respect, regardless of what you've gone through or how you're feeling as a result. Factors such as patriarchy and White supremacy keep us from extending empathy to those who are harmed, or from rightfully receiving that empathy and support. If somebody is in pain, they deserve belief, support, and care.

Wolf's story also brings up the point that, for some of us who engage in BDSM, it can seem as though everybody that you talk to has trauma. This is a common conversation that I've seen within the BDSM and kink community. However, there is no higher incidence of abuse history in the kink community when compared to the larger population. Because BDSM deals with our sexuality and the different things that have happened to us and because consent in negotiation are the bedrock and foundation of BDSM, conversations about abuse, trauma, and other difficulties are going to come up more frequently. In the larger culture, we tend not to talk about these things or have welcoming spaces to do so, and so in the greater population, many people who have trauma stay silent. The Adverse Childhood Experiences (ACE) study, which investigated the impact of difficult events early in one's life, shows that some 61 percent of adults surveyed across twenty-five states reported having at least one type of ACE and nearly one in six reported having endured four or more types. In addition, women and numerous ethnic minority groups were at a higher risk for four-plus types of early adversity. In other words, a history of trauma is common in and outside the BDSM and kink community. A related myth worth mentioning is that because someone was abused by someone of their same sex or gender, that can lead them to "become" gay, lesbian, or transgender. That's simply not how sexual orientation or gender work, nor has any correlation between these factors been found.

What we do know is that sexual trauma can lead to sexual activities or interactions being activating at times. Signals we receive from our body during arousal or pleasure may remind us of traumatic events, and it can be difficult for the body to determine whether we're in the painful past or a safer present. While all of this can feel understandably confusing, we can take steps to better manage trauma and any reactions we might experience and step more fully into accepting and embracing pleasure if or when we feel ready.

Grounding Exercise

Hold onto a comforting or interesting object. Maybe it's a special stone, a silky scarf, or a meaningful charm. Close your eyes, if that helps you hone in on the object. Breathe deeply as you pay attention to and really notice with your hands (and eyes, if they remain open and you're able) all of the different textures and parts. To bring your focus deeper, say what you're noticing aloud. Take your time and remember to breathe as is most comfortable for you.

4
"I Need Help."

I need help. These three little words are some of the bravest and most important ones you can admit to yourself or a loved one when you're dealing with trauma's aftermath. Before you read on, please take a moment to consider how tremendous that accomplishment is. You chose this book, and you're reading this section. Those steps alone show that you're courageous and worthy.

There's also nothing shameful about feeling challenged or over-whelmed by recognizing the need for help or about seeking it. Trauma and factors that often exist along with it, such as mental illness, neuro-divergence, and low self-esteem, can all make clarity around these issues difficult. *Are we really struggling with something that requires outside help? Shouldn't we be able to figure this out for ourselves?* When these kinds of questions arise, the answers are that we probably *do* need support and, *no*, we shouldn't be expected to sort things out alone. And regardless, support around challenges is always a good thing.

As you get started toward seeking help, selecting your best option, or options, may draw up a range of emotions, from excitement or nervousness to "OMG, now what?" The process of finding a thera-pist when you've been feeling frequently or consistently triggered, for example, can feel emotionally draining, adding to your ongoing state of being overwhelmed. Where do you go? And how do you even go about it when you're in the midst of feeling frequently or perpetually awful? Our executive function tends to suffer amid trauma flares, so even the simplest tasks of making phone calls or going over a calendar can feel intense.

As with seeking help for other kinds of challenges, there is no one type of trauma-related support that's ideal, or even helpful, for everyone. The same mindfulness practice or talk therapy that helps one person immeasurably might help another only mildly or even bring on lingering distress. While the idea of "trial and error" can feel scary, deeply frustrating, or both when you're hoping to better manage trauma, there are ways to make the process easier.

As you consider various options, guide with what resonates most with you. Does a particular type of therapy or a certain provider give you even a mild sense of curiosity and hope? Even if you're not quite sure why, trusting your instincts may prove helpful. Meanwhile, consider seeking support from one or more loved ones who can help hold you accountable or even make phone calls on your behalf. You could text or email a close friend, for example, and say, "Hey, I'm hoping to get started with therapy and the process feels pretty challenging. Would you mind checking in with me on Friday?" or "Could you come by on Saturday afternoon to sit with me while I make phone calls?"

As you peruse provider websites, if you notice that someone you're interested in potentially working with provides an initial low- or no-cost consultation, take them up on that. These consultations often take place by phone and can help give you a sense as to whether or not you're well-suited to work together, based on factors such as your comfort level. Beforehand, make a list of questions you may have, as well as your priorities. Is it important for you to have a therapist who shares your ethnicity or gender? Or one who specializes not only in trauma but in another area of mental health?

And also important, if you begin a form of treatment and at any point it doesn't feel like a good fit, know that there are almost always more options. Discuss your feelings with the provider, if you feel comfortable doing so. (If you don't feel comfortable speaking freely, that may be a red flag.) A trustworthy, professional provider won't take offense or judge you for seeking support that better fits your needs elsewhere. Most will respect your preferences, and all will ideally respect your needs. They may even offer support, such as providing referrals, as you navigate your next best steps.

TYPES OF TRAUMA TREATMENT

All trauma-focused therapy treatments aim to help you better manage trauma, and each form and provider is unique. And in many cases, a provider weaves in one or more types into what's also known collectively as trauma therapy. Regardless of the form you choose, make sure the treatment is provided by an experienced and properly credentialed professional who is either trauma-informed or provides trauma-focused care. Some of the main options include:

Behavioral Therapy

Behavioral therapy aims to help you change potentially self-destructive or otherwise unhealthy behaviors. The most common form involves exposure therapy, during which you gradually face your fears without the dreaded consequence occurring. The exposure might use your imagination or actual exposure during therapy, or systematic desensitization, where gradually increased exposure is paired with relaxation.

This form of therapy is considered by many to be effective for treating PTSD when trauma-focused care is prioritized and education provided. Research findings are mixed, however, with some showing that symptoms remain after treatment.

Cognitive Behavioral Therapy

Cognitive behavioral therapy (CBT) aims to change incorrect thoughts while increasing your skills and knowledge. During this treatment, you might learn breathing exercises to help manage stress and anxiety and gain education about normal reactions to trauma. Your provider will also help you identify and evaluate negative and "irrational" thoughts, guiding you toward replacing them with more accurate ones. CBT may involve exposure therapy too.

Dialectical Behavior Therapy

Dialectical behavior therapy (DBT) aims to help you feel more grounded in your life and increase a sense of self-control. Originally developed in the 1980s as a treatment for borderline personality disorder, it's since been found helpful for managing the effects of trauma, especially in people living with PTSD. DBT is founded on Zen Buddhist practices and philosophies. "Dialectical," for example, refers to a synthesis of opposites, which is at the core of Zen practices. It also emphasizes "radical acceptance" of who you are as a means of stimulating growth and healing.

Group Therapy

Group therapy is exactly what it sounds like: therapy in a group setting. Appropriate groups provide coping skills and education while focusing on self-care and cultivating connection between others. Group therapy tends to be the most effective when it's paired with individual therapy and approved or recommended by your primary therapist. Psychodynamic group therapy with a relational approach may be an especially useful option if you feel harmed by a lack of community or external acceptance, such as for newly arrived migrants experiencing insecure attachment, grief, and isolation.

Psychodynamic Therapy

Psychodynamic therapy strives to identify which phase of traumatic responses you're stuck in. Once your therapist determines that, they'll figure out which aspects of the root(s) of that trauma interfere with your ability to process and manage it. Your treatment will likely take your childhood development into account, prioritize your under-standing of the trauma, and examine ways the trauma has impacted your sense of self, your life quality, and your relationships.

Pharmacotherapy

Pharmacotherapy aims to disrupt traumatic reactions through use of medications. Medications may also help manage coexisting con-ditions, such as depression, anxiety, or ADHD, which can contrib-ute to trauma and make its effects more challenging. Medications may be useful for reducing trauma-related symptoms such as intru-sive thoughts, hypervigilance, irritability, emotional reactivity, and insomnia, either temporarily or long term. Your therapist might recommend seeing a psychiatrist about medication use as part of your overall treatment plan, particularly if other means of treatment aren't sufficient.

When speaking to your primary care physician or psychiatrist, it's a good idea to bring notes with you if you think you may forget to say something important and to write down what happens during the appointment so you can refer back to it later. Also, because the appointments can be short, focus on the following to get the most out of that time:

- Share the specific symptoms that you are experiencing.
- Share how long you've been experiencing them.
- Share how severe the symptoms are/how much they are interfering in your life (personally, socially, and occupationally).

Often, we may have had too many experiences of not getting the support we need. There is the undeniable fact that racism and other types of systemic discrimination actively harm or interfere specifically with Black people getting proper care. Additionally, we might feel shame that we are having emotional difficulties and therefore downplay the severity of our suffering. Don't minimize your hurt. Please do advocate for your wellness. If needed, ask around and change providers if you feel that you are not getting the care you deserve. Bring a trusted person to medical appointments if you can. Additionally, let the physician know about your life and family history. This includes sharing information about any family history of emotional disturbances, and any supplements or other substances you are taking. And if you are having unpleasant side effects from a prescription medication, bring this to your medical provider's attention. Many providers truly want to help, and to do that they need the fullest amount of information you can give them.

Trauma-Informed or Trauma-Focused Sex Therapy

Trauma-informed sex therapy can help you navigate the effects of trauma that interfere with not only your life, but also your sexuality and intimate relationships. Sessions are somatically focused and targeted around helping you feel safe in your body, and they can help you stay aware of and navigate struggles around sex, which may be activating. The therapist will give information about sexual functioning and methods to enhance pleasure. This psychoeducation weaves in how to slow down, communicate, and maintain awareness of somatic responses while pushing against societal narratives about how our bodies are supposed to respond and how our relationships are supposed to be. Our sex lives and relationships become a place of liberation because they're separated from the societal stories. Trauma-*focused* sex therapy, on the other hand, is a much more specific treatment modality that's helpful when you've endured severe sexual or physical abuse. Treatments may be more in depth and longer lasting.

Somatic Therapy

Somatic therapy focuses on your physical sensations and where trauma "lives" or is experienced in your body. The word *somatic* derives from the Greek word *soma*, which means "living body." Your provider will help you become more aware of these sensations, working with the premises that trauma affects the autonomic nervous system and that the mind and body are deeply connected. In doing so, it aims to help you (and your body) reframe traumas for a stronger sense of self. Types of somatic therapy include sensorimotor therapy, created by Pat Ogden, the Hakomi Method, relational Gestalt, and somatic experiencing.

Art Therapy and Music Therapy

Art therapy and music therapy can both utilize creative expression to help you examine and unpack emotions and share details of trauma experiences that may be difficult to articulate through words alone. Your trauma-specializing therapist may discuss your emotions and experiences with you as you paint, draw, or play an instrument. Some people find that the sensory stimulation provides responses linked with familiarity, comfort, and security in times of crisis.

Equine-Assisted Psychotherapy and Therapy Animals

Equine-assisted therapy uses nonverbal communication and connection between you and a horse to re-form positive relationships with people, bring a sense of relaxation, and instill coping skills such as asking for and receiving help, so you can regain a sense of control. Therapy animals may also be an option for some people with PTSD or related issues, such as anxiety, related to trauma. (While it's not considered a treatment, many people find the companionship of a pet to be therapeutic as well.)

SUPPLEMENTAL TREATMENTS

Many therapies considered to be "alternative" or nontraditional provide tremendous healing for survivors of trauma. Unfortunately, they tend to be less often covered by insurance. Because some of these treatments aren't regulated the same way as conventional therapies, consider discussing their use with your primary therapist or physician before starting. Referrals in this case may be especially useful. If you have access and/or conventional treatments haven't been helpful or sufficient on their own, you may find one or more of the following modalities helpful:

Cannabidiol

Cannabidiol, or CBD, is the active ingredient in hemp, a cousin of the marijuana plant. Available in various forms, such as liquid tincture, oils, edibles, and vapes, it's commonly used to address insomnia and anxiety. A case study showed its benefits for reducing anxiety and sleep disruptions associated with PTSD. While CBD is legal in most states, it can interact with certain medications and have varying impacts on people. So far, no "most effective" therapeutic dose is known, but it's generally considered safe.

Eye Movement and Desensitization and Reprocessing

Eye movement and desensitization and reprocessing (EMDR) involves focusing on a negative belief about yourself or a traumatic experience while shifting your eyes from side to side, typically following a moving light or object. It may also involve sounds that shift from one side of headphones to the other. This process is believed to help by changing neural pathways associated with traumatic memories so they can be desensitized or reframed. The process often involves trauma-focused talk therapy, grounding exercises, and/or somatic work too.

Hypnotherapy

Hypnotherapy uses guided relaxation and intense concentration to help you achieve a bolstered sense of awareness. This "trance" or hypnotic state is meant to allow you to block out attention on anything besides what your provider guides you through, potentially making analysis more feasible. When traumatic details are revealed in greater detail, you then discuss them with an appropriate therapist. (Because a harmful minority of practitioners lead people to create false memories, finding a highly qualified provider is exceptionally important.)

Psychedelics

Many scientists and practitioners successfully treated psychological difficulties with psychedelics until they were banned in 1970. Lately, they've been resurfacing in mainstream culture, with clinical trials and pilot studies of medically supervised LSD, ketamine, psilocybin, and MDMA showing benefits for people living with alcoholism, opiate addiction, anxiety, depression, and PTSD. Psychedelics may help by allowing you to recall a painful memory without visceral trauma reactions, such as fight, flight, or freeze. It's important to note that people of color, particularly Black, Latinx, and Asian folks, are very underrepresented in psychedelic studies and more inclusive recruitment techniques are vital, as is greater accessibility to these treatments in these populations.

GLORIA: DIFFERENT (NOT BROKEN) AND SEX-POSITIVE THERAPY

Growing up, Gloria Jackson-Nefertiti knew she was different from her peers. And if she had had any doubt, the frequent bullying would have made it known. Other kids made fun of her because she didn't "talk proper," she said. While they all spoke with a southern accent, her words came out in a "formal, almost stilted fashion," with no hint of the accent, despite the fact that she lived in Mississippi from birth until age fifteen. "I was so different from the other children and never fit in with them," she said. "It was very common for them to laugh at whatever I'd say." The bullying continued at home, she added, along with other forms of emotional and physical abuse by her late father.

Gloria's already dwindling self-esteem took a further dive starting around age forty, after she met a man named Artie at a poly pot-luck, whom she would go on to stay partnered with for close to two decades. Artie turned out to be a "racist bully with incredible sexual shame," she said, and he treated her as though she were "only good for sex." "I didn't realize until close to the end of the relationship . . . that he never [acted as though he] liked me, constantly found fault with me, and regularly pointed out what was 'wrong' with me," she recalled. "The only area where he found no fault with me whatso-ever was the area of sex. He couldn't seem to praise me enough for that!"

Now in her early sixties, Gloria realizes there was never anything "wrong" with her. More than most anything else, she credits her work with a sex-positive, poly-friendly, kink-friendly, and LGBTQ-friendly therapist for her ongoing growth and healing. After sessions with a therapist who didn't seem to understand her polyamorous lifestyle, and instead often blamed challenges she faced on having more than one partner, she knew she had to find a better fit. Once she did, virtually everything shifted for the better.

In 2018 her current therapist helped identify something about Gloria that she had needed to understand for decades: that she has autism spectrum disorder. "I was telling her about something that happened at home with my housemates . . . some kind of misunderstanding that is really common when you have autism, because we process information differently from other people," she said, noting that these types of misunderstandings are especially common when dealing with written communication, such as email and social media, where facial expressions are absent. "And my therapist said, 'Well, you know, I assess people for autism.' And so I told her I would definitely be interested in being assessed."

Learning that she is autistic brought Gloria a sense of grief initially, as she looked back on her life wondering how different many aspects would have been had she known that she wasn't "flawed" or "broken" after all, and that she instead had a disorder with a name and ways to manage it. The diagnosis also felt empowering, though, so much so that Gloria now tells everyone she can that she's autistic. "I remember when I was first in the process of going through the assessment with my therapist, I posted something about it on Facebook, and somebody had said, 'You know, I really can't imagine that you have autism.' And remarks like that just kind of prove how important it is for me to get the word out and let people know right away that I'm autistic."

If Gloria had known that autism can manifest in people the way it does in her, she might have gained her current level of self-awareness, confidence, and support earlier on, a gap that has fueled her trauma. Her outspokenness is especially important for fellow African American women, given that autism is often overlooked or diagnosed later among children and adults in many non-White ethnic populations. Her therapist has also helped her process other sources of trauma and navigate a breast cancer diagnosis in 2013, allowing her to thrive in a myriad of ways.

The experience with breast cancer "really changed everything," Gloria said, particularly paired with the self-work and helpful therapy she had started by then. "I started to love myself and stop caring what other people thought, because what happened was the diagnosis showed me how short life is. . . . I realized that I had no reason to care what people thought of me and that I was going to just be out as bisexual, polyamorous, and sex-positive."

All of that culminated in a workshop called Transcending Shame that Gloria created and started teaching at conferences in 2017. "Before that happened, I really don't see how I could have led the workshop, because I'm really vulnerable in the class. I go through a lot of personal examples. If I were still worrying about what people thought . . . there's no way I could do that. And by being open like this, it certainly helps other people see that they're not alone."

In sharing her journey, Gloria hopes others who are managing trauma will feel encouraged to seek the support they deserve and need. And if the first provider you find has values that vary from yours or lacks a specialization you would find most helpful, keep looking. "I can't emphasize enough the importance of having a good therapist," she said, adding that finding a sex-positive, LGBTQIA+-friendly therapist is especially important if you're not a straight, monogamous person. "That way, you can be completely honest in your sessions and not have to hide or have to explain your sexual and relationship orientation to your therapist." The last thing we need while managing trauma is to feel judged by the very people we seek help from.

NADIA: DAY PROGRAMS, GROUP THERAPY, AND SETTLING INTO LOVE

Nadia said she finds it nearly impossible to relax in sexual situations. She has a tendency to become hypersexual for the first month or so of relationships before her ability to engage in sex suddenly halts. Her desire for sex meets what she describes as a "shutting down," and this reaction has ruined numerous relationships.

These sexual difficulties emerged during her relationship with her high school boyfriend, but they were hard to sort out, given that she had no idea what sex even entailed at that point. And like many people who endure sexual trauma during childhood, an all too common lack of comprehensive sex education kept her from grasping exactly what had happened to her at age eleven, when she was raped repeatedly by her brother for about a year. Emotionally abusive parents and messaging from the fundamentalist Christian church she grew up in sourced her trauma too.

When she was nineteen, the year after she and her first boyfriend broke up, Nadia attempted suicide and nearly died. She then spent several stints in a psychiatric ward, totaling seven months. She could leave perhaps permanently, the program directors offered, if she would commit to attending a day program. She accepted, and the nonspecific group therapy in these programs turned out to be her most helpful form of treatment.

"Everyone is there because of fucked-up shit, but the point of the groups is to provide structure in the day more than anything else," she said, adding that opportunities to talk in vague terms about trauma (specifics were discouraged) to people who related, empathized, and could summarize what she meant, helped hugely—far more so than individual therapy, where she didn't "do so well." At the day program, she could say something like, "I don't even know why I do X, I just have to because if I don't then . . ." and then shrug. Someone would then reply, "I totally know what you mean. Sometimes it feels like this pressure building in you, at first maybe just in your belly or whatever but then it spreads to your chest and your head and even your arms and legs until you can't think, you can't feel, you just need to get it out before you explode," and so on. Meanwhile, Nadia would sit there in awe, she recalled, "going, 'Yeah, that's exactly what it's like.'"

Heavily drinking, self-harming, and still engaging in suicidal behaviors while living alone made having somewhere safe to go, where folks would check on her and keep her alive, essential. "The more I went, the more I bonded with other people there," she said, "and that was really helpful too—especially on hard nights where I wasn't sure I was gonna make it. Sometimes I would think, 'I only have to make it four more hours, then I can leave for group. It'll be Tuesday, so this person will be there, or we're doing that activity I wanted to do.'"

Nadia described one of the art programs she participated in as a structured psychotherapy group where members would talk about the art they created on a given day, which was usually based on a theme that arose in a previous talk session. "I did find it surprisingly helpful, even if I didn't like sharing in group what [my art] was really about," she noted. "They found it really frustrating having me there because I never talked about myself [or] my own stuff, but I learned a lot just from doing the activities or listening in and contributing to others, and the art was a huge part of that for me."

This tendency to not talk about herself is one reason individual therapy felt like a mismatch for Nadia. Whereas in groups, she could sit quietly, learn from others' shares, and contribute thoughts more sparingly. "With one-on-one therapy I feel a lot of pressure to talk about things I don't want to or am not ready to, and even when I just have to listen to what the psychologist or whoever is saying, I find it hard to focus because all of their attention is on me," she explained. "You would think growing up in such a big family that having someone's undivided attention would be nice, but the only times that happened growing up was when you were separated from the group for individual punishment, or in my case also for other abuse. So I generally feel safer in a group."

Now, a decade or so since her first suicide attempt, Nadia is in a stable relationship with a married couple, which she described as "amazing." Realizing a few years ago that she doesn't have to be in a "traditional" relationship with just one person has been positive and impactful in her life. Once that epiphany struck, she knew polyamory was what she wanted to settle down into. "The relationship side of things is going really well, but the sex side of things is still a bit of a problem," she said. "Thankfully both my partners are super understanding, and my girlfriend has a history of abuse, too, so we are pretty aware of how that impacts each of us."

Her boyfriend, who has a fairly high libido compared to Nadia and her girlfriend, "sorts himself out," relying on tools such as porn when the others aren't sex inclined. And when he and Nadia have sex, it tends to be focused on his pleasure, a decision she makes. She finds it easier to relax during sex with her girlfriend and described sexual intimacy with both partners at the same time as "amazing and lots of fun, and probably the most relaxed [she gets] in intimate situations." It may not happen very often, she said, but she savors it when it does.

While Nadia grapples with wishing she desired sex more frequently and not knowing how to get there, she has become much better at communicating her wants and needs. All in all, she said, "being in a relationship where I have evidence that I can say 'no' and 'that's OK' and it doesn't change the whole dynamic of the relationship has been a huge part of that growth in terms of being able to be more relaxed when I do have sex, so hopefully that continues in an upward trend."

Although her life would have been very different without childhood sexual trauma, Nadia is grateful that it essentially forced her to seek support. In doing so, she's ended up processing numerous additional abuses she's endured, which have manifested "a lot more quietly and insidiously," and for which she would never have sought treatment. Therapy has allowed her to learn a great deal about herself, ways to navigate challenges in her relationships related to emotional abuse she endured, and how to openly communicate with partners. This is an ongoing learning process, she said, but she can now "do it reliably enough that we can muddle our way through instead of just quitting."

Jamila's Reflections

Both Gloria's and Nadia's stories illustrate that finding the right therapist/therapeutic frame can make all the difference. Given that trauma work is about helping to restore a sense of connection and regulation within yourself and with others, it's critical that the therapeutic frame supports who you are and what you need. This doesn't mean that support can or should mimic your exact demographic or identities. Although there are more and more different kinds of clinicians entering the field each year, there are no immediate "perfect matches." As with any relationship, we deserve to be with people with whom we can grow and change *and* who can meet us where we are. For Gloria, having a therapist who could focus on three of the aspects that are critical parts of her identity (being autistic, nonmonogamous, and bisexual) allowed her to explore and integrate these aspects and move forward. For Nadia, safety and learning happens within a more expanded framework of groups. This allowed her to participate in her own way, notice themes and patterns, and incorporate the feeling of interconnection into her life.

GINNY AND JEAN: GRIEF, COMMUNICATION, AND SAFER SELF-HELP

Kirby Brown was an adventurer, according to her mother, Ginny Brown, the "kind of person who just sort of fills the room when she walks in." She loved to dance, she loved music, and she was just "very alive." Or, as Ginny often puts it, "drunk on life." "She was a real gatherer in the family as well, always thinking of vacations and bringing us together," Ginny added. "She was the one who would call my other three children to say, 'It's Mom's birthday,' or 'It's Mom and Dad's anniversary.' She was very thoughtful."

In October 2009, Ginny received the worst news a parent can hear. Kirby had died. It seemed unfathomable, especially given that Kirby was at something as benign as a spiritual self-help retreat. How could there be anything violent or fatal about that? She would soon learn that the event and the "guru" at its head were indeed that dangerous. That man, James Arthur Ray, was famously part of *The Secret*, the book turned self-help craze that focuses on the Law of Attraction and swept the nation after its release in 2006. "Kirby was very attracted to everything Oprah," Ginny said. "And Oprah has done some wonderful things, don't get me wrong. But when *The Secret* came out and Oprah was all about *The Secret*, Kirby and her painting partner in the Baja were very excited about *The Secret* and wanted all their friends to read the book and watch the DVD. And that's when she first saw James Ray and then he was down in the Baja for an introductory meet-and-greet kind of thing."

From there, Kirby seemed hooked. The welcoming man boasted a mighty charisma and spoke with a sense of deep authority. He seemed like a great teacher who synthesized different Eastern and Western philosophies with science to help others grow and thrive. Only later would Kirby's family learn that the training and background he spoke of were false, which made the "science" he touted questionable as well.

At the time, Kirby really wanted to expand her decorative painting business to make it more mainstream, Ginny said, versus applying her keen artistic abilities largely to painting mansions on the Sea of Cortez as she had been. After walking away from a series of disappointing relationships, Kirby also longed to find a befitting life partner. That longing for the proverbial "something more" is what leads many people to self-help groups and events, particularly those led by people who seem to possess a higher level of being. And while these options can be understandably appealing, too many provide something more along the lines of other-help, assisting the person or people at its front the most, allowing them to become better known, wealthier, or both, sometimes at a great cost to members and followers. When these groups are experiential, they're also known as large-group awareness training, or LGAT. These groups tend to use unconventional and often risky means of increasing self-awareness, and promise incredible personal transformation, over the course of several days. A dynamic leader may stand before a crowded room that buzzes with excitement, creating an evangelical church–like feel. That leader and their team might lead you through activities designed to "break you down" or "break through barriers" using a range of techniques. Some people benefit from these events. Many others are harmed in some way.

On October 8, 2009, at Ray's "Spiritual Warrior" retreat in Sedona, Arizona, Kirby and two other attendees, James Shore and Liz Neuman, died during a sweat lodge challenge, one that they were told in advance might lead them to feel as though they might die. Not only had that seed of to-be-expected deathlike sensations been planted, one that could easily prompt someone to stay in a dangerous situation, but the extreme heat of a misused and irresponsibly constructed—not to mention culturally appropriated—sweat lodge could alter your rational thinking. "I always think, if Kirby had really understood sensory deprivation, maybe she would have been more conscious of the fact that her own decision-making power was impaired by the time she got to the end of the week," Ginny said.

After Kirby died, the family gathered together to talk openly about what had happened and how they were feeling. As a trauma-informed licensed clinical social worker, Ginny knew that bringing light to and communicating about everyone's emotions were vital—as did her husband, George, who also worked in the mental health field and had a clinical understanding of trauma. "I think one of the things George did that was kind of extraordinary was as soon as the entire family was together, he did what is essentially a critical incident debriefing," Ginny recalled. "He got everyone together in the living room and said, 'OK, this happened Thursday night. We're finally all here together. . . . What are you thinking? How do you feel? What did you hear today? What sense did you make out of that?' So there was a lot of talking from the very beginning."

Every night for the week and a half they were all together, the whole family would gather to talk. Then after the kids were in bed, Ginny and George would continue the conversation in bed for a good two hours. "One night, we just talked about how angry we were at Kirby," Ginny said. "And I think that's a piece of grieving that people don't do, because you're not supposed to be angry at the person who's passed. But we were furious with her: *Why did you not think you were enough? Why did you feel you had to believe this guy? Why didn't you get out of the tent? Why didn't you realize you were in danger?* So we spent a lot of time screaming and cursing at her. And then a lot of time expressing our anger at both what happened and also with [Ray]." Understanding that these emotions are real and that they have to be expressed so that they can be not erased, but managed, have been essential for her family's ability to cope.

On their way to Kirby's funeral, Ginny told the children, "Don't let your anger and your incredible sadness . . . don't let that destroy you. Because if you do, he will have taken another victim." Ginny recognizes that there is no such thing as closure in a tragedy such as losing a child. Rather, she said, "It's a question of learning how to figure out how to allow it to be incorporated into your life in a way that you're not blowing yourself up."

Within weeks of Kirby's death, the family knew they wanted to do something to honor Kirby's life. From there blossomed SEEK Safely Inc., a nonprofit organization that educates the public about the self-help industry through a website, public presentations, and ongoing research. Unlike other industries, such as mental health and medicine, there are no official regulations or safety standards in place in the self-help field. Anyone can proclaim themselves an expert and practice as they so choose. And while there are helpful individuals in the community, it can be difficult to sort them out from the potentially harmful options, especially during raw, vulnerable times.

Kirby's sister, Jean Brown, said she especially wanted to help create SEEK Safely because if Kirby had survived, she's certain she would have championed it. "She would have been one of the people who was really speaking out about how messed up it was that happened," she said. "And so I think that she would be happy with what we're doing. I think she would be proud. . . . She would have started this organization."

Jamila's Reflections

Kirby's story is nothing short of heartbreaking. This is a person who loved her life, cared deeply about other people, and wanted to contribute, to the best of her ability, her skills and talents to the world and that was taken from her. The world holds so much pain and so many of us are trying to find a way out and a way through it, not just for our own sake but because we want to help others. Tragically, there are unscrupulous and uncaring people who will exploit those desires for their own personal or financial gain. And I do not give the mental health industry exemption from this. There are therapists, as well as self-help guides and "gurus," who do not have the individual's wellness in mind.

In the culture we live in, which prizes self-actualization, encourages exceptionalism, encourages us to create wealth, and links wealth with morality, so many messages suggest that if you have youth and money and health and "good looks," that you are a morally good person. While this is seldom expressed explicitly, it is woven into this culture, creating a dangerous situation, particularly for people who had or continue to have systemic abuse and power leveraged against them or who've been injured by abuse within their family of origin or other systems in which they should have been safe. They are aiming to try to get better. But in trying to heal themselves, they're also primed for predators to take advantage of them. I cannot stress enough how critical it is to learn the signs of your body, to learn when it feels safe, to learn when it feels in danger, to learn when it's experiencing something that is about wellness and pleasure, when it's frightened, when it feels challenged, but still safe. It is critical to listen to the language of your body, so that when—not if, but when—you come across people who seek to exploit you, something in your body has awareness of what is happening. And if you can find a way to then get away from those people, you could well save your life.

I have such respect for Kirby's mother and father for sharing their pain and anger toward Kirby, because we cannot allow ourselves to be trapped by narrow definitions of obligation, convention, "shoulds," or notions that "you're not supposed to speak ill of the dead" or that you are supposed to simply "move on." These ideas obscure our actual feelings and prevent us from understanding our varied feelings during the mourning process. When a violation occurs, when we learn that the world is not the safe place it should be, when someone dies, we will never see the world the same way as before. But if we are to move to acceptance and ultimately toward integration, then we must allow space for the storms of our grief. The fact that Kirby's parents could speak to their anger and helplessness around Kirby's choices and her death speaks to their courage and their love for Kirby. They have allowed space for the variety of feelings that come up around their child and the many facets there are in the grieving process. It would be a disservice to Kirby's life and Kirby's contributions to speak of her only in connection to her death. Although the manner of her passing is a painful but important cautionary story, we hope that you think of her as a full person, a complex person, and that she deserved to have a life in which she could explore new ideas. She did not need to be "perfect" to deserve comfort, truth, and a safe environment in which to explore herself.

In your search for healing, in your search for reclamation of your past and a new way forward, there will be many people who will step forward to tell you they have the way through, the way to help you get a better life and all of the things you could have ever wanted. What I want most for you is to realize *nobody can sell you back to yourself.* Nobody can sell you into understanding the crevices of your soul, all of the unique rivulets and currents of who you are. The best people will give you an environment to figure that out for yourself; they will make room, facilitate your sense of self-discovery, and foster your ability to create community around you. That is what we hope you find: people who simply create a caring structure and then allow you the space to create that which you are seeking.

Be wary of those who seem to have all the answers. Life is uncertain. It is precarious. It changes. There are so many things to discover along the way that we could never have known at the outset. All I can offer to you, all we can offer to you, are practices to help you navigate it all—no clear answers, just simply the knowledge that you're not alone and that there are certain ways of being that will move you closer to that which you are seeking. There is no path, program, or organization that can grant you awareness of who you are. You are the expert on yourself and following your curiosity, following your pleasure, following what your principles tell you, following all of that to the end, *that* is your life. And there is something profoundly beautiful, imperfect, and phenomenal about that. Don't let anyone take that from you.

"SELF-HELP" RED FLAGS TO LOOK OUT FOR
Hard Sales Tactics

Pushiness is not helpful when you're working to improve your own life, especially while you're managing trauma. It's also a common sign of impending harm. Jean said a definite red flag is "when you get a really strong sense of the hard sales tactics like scarcity, you know, 'There are only ten spots left at this next event. You have to sign up now or you're going to miss your spot!'" Coercive sales techniques are bad signs as well, she added, "where they're saying, 'You know, if you're really serious about changing your life, if you *really mean it*, if you *really* want this, you're going to buy the next program or buy the book series or whatever.'" Feeling pressured in those ways does nothing to help you help yourself, and more often occurs as a tactic designed to sell programs versus truly supporting others.

A Lack of Transparency

Any ethical, caring professional who truly wants you to be able to improve your life will be upfront about answering any questions you might have, from inquiring about fees or requesting referrals to asking what exactly will happen or what you can expect at a particular event. If the person or organization tries to uphold a sense of "mystery" rather than respectfully address your concerns, changes the subject, ignores you, or, worst of all, insults you in some way (e.g., "You must not really be ready"), move along. Ideally, the provider of a self-help product or service will clearly list details, such as pricing, publicly on their website.

Questionable or Unverifiable Credentials

There are many types of education, and not every helpful expert has academic letters after their name. What you want to avoid is working with someone who isn't honest about their background or whose background doesn't give them the experience or authority to teach you what they claim to know. Before investing in a self-help program, find out where the leader gained their expertise. Did they learn from personal experience? Or study at a particular school? And those credentials should be verifiably legitimate. "It's one thing to tell an inspirational story and give that to people and say, you know, 'Take from it what you will,'" Jean said. "But it's another thing when you start really dispensing advice that you don't have a background in." This can be difficult to sort out, given that some of the most harmful self-proclaimed gurus are known to make up credentials or leverage credentials that they obtained in a completely different field than the one they're currently operating in.

A "God" or "Hero" Complex

True self-help is meant to empower you to help yourself, said Jean, by providing tools you can apply in your life, without making you dependent on the program. If a group is hyperfocused on its figurehead who touts a lot more charm and charisma than transparency or verifiable skills and background, that's a warning sign. SEEK Safely asks self-help providers to sign a commitment to being truthful about their credentials and to providing accurate information. "This may sound ridiculous, but it never occurred to me that someone was going to get up on stage and lie about how many years they have trained, how many people they had worked with," Ginny remarked. "How do you lie in front of hundreds and hundreds of people? Like, really? Aren't you going to get found out? It's mind-boggling."

Grandiose Promises or "The Only Way"

Similar to the "God" or "hero" complex, the information provided by a self-help program or provider should respect that different steps and methods work for different people. If they seem to suggest "my way or the highway" or trash talk conventional support (i.e., "psychiatric medications are dangerous," "therapy doesn't work," or "suicide help-lines aren't helpful"), they are already doing more harm than good. And much like the diet and weight loss industry, the most harmful programs make unrealistic claims, such as a particular book, event, or group "is guaranteed to change your life!" Particularly for better managing trauma, there is no "one way" or "quick fix" method—and suggesting that proven, clinical means of support aren't helpful is outright dangerous.

Trust Your Instincts . . . When You Can

It can be difficult to differentiate between residual effects of trauma and your "inner voice" or "gut instinct," which is important and trust-worthy *when you're able to discern the difference*. "If someone is rela-tively healthy and they have an interior radar when something is off, and you get that kind of feeling, you need to pay attention to it," said Ginny. "If someone has been seriously traumatized in their history and that internal protective instinct has been damaged, because for years they've been told, 'Oh, no, that's not what happened,' and that internal protective system has been really screwed around with, then it's hard for them to be able to trust their instincts. They may still have the instinct, but . . . they've been trained to not trust it." If you feel too scared or intimidated to leave a program once you've joined, that's another cue worth listening to.

Don't hesitate to ask someone trustworthy to help you sort this all out. And if you feel stubborn or defensive about needing to start a particular program now, without taking time to think things through or to seek help in finding your best option, that's a good indication that slowing down and seeking that support may be exactly what you need.

Grounding Exercise

Distract yourself. Sometimes mindfulness and presence aren't what you need in a triggered or activated moment. Give yourself permission to distract yourself from your ruminating, anxious, or otherwise uncomfortable thoughts. (If you can't fully distract yourself, that's OK. Simply aim to focus on something else as well.) Scroll Instagram using one of your favorite uplifting hashtags. Count backward from twenty, fifty, or one hundred. Or sing a silly song out loud. If movement helps you, walk around, stretch your arms from side to side, or dance in place as you count or sing.

5
"I Am Such a Problem."

Shame. This insidious creature rears its head often among many survivors navigating trauma and triggers. Sociologist Brené Brown defines shame as "the intensely painful feeling or experience of believing that we are flawed and therefore unworthy of love and belonging." Whereas guilt stems from doing something wrong, shame says, *we are wrong*—typically meaning flawed or unworthy. When we are activated by triggers and those feelings affect people we care about, it's all too easy to blame ourselves, even though we did not ask for the trauma to occur, nor do we endure its impact by choice. It's as though we blame ourselves for struggling: if I were stronger/smarter/more capable or more *fill-in-the-blank*, I wouldn't "ruin" or "hurt" another's life. But you are not a burden to be fixed, or shunned, or blamed. The courage it takes to go about life as someone who has gone through a trauma event, or series of events, makes you quite the opposite. And that is just one of your countless attributes that prove you are not only worthy of love and acceptance, but a spectacular human being.

Believing otherwise about yourself may take a variety of forms, in terms of language. Other common expressions of "I am such a problem" include:

"I am broken."

"I should be better at handling this."

"I am hurting my partner."

"I don't know why, but I don't want my partner(s) around me."

"I mess everything up."

"I wish I wanted sex more often."

"I wish they didn't have to deal with me."

"I'm uncontrollable."

"I wish I didn't do these 'strange' things."

"I'm confusing my partner(s)."

These types of thoughts don't crop up out of nowhere. And none of us were born with a natural tendency to experience deep shame related to trauma. We were, however, taught to. In response to our understandable traumatic feelings, Western cultures, particularly the United States, invest large amounts of money into telling us that if we really want growth and positivity in our lives, all we have to do is *think positive!* (And buy magical programs and products that promise to teach us just how.) We need not be held back by our past, the "gurus" tell us. *Let us break free!* When we hear and absorb these prevalent messages, how can we *not* wonder or believe that we are completely fucking up? Cultural, familial, and religious messages about needing to be a "good girl" or "strong boy," avoid crying, remain as "productive" as possible, present only specific and limited types of sexuality, gender, and relationships, avoid pleasures such as rich food, and forgive the unforgivable also fuel these feelings. Whether we absorbed these ideas during childhood or later on, they can linger and pose problems, most so if we don't recognize them, which is easy to do in today's world.

For survivors of trauma, the self-shame that can stem up around feeling triggered and resultantly "broken" can become another form of trauma on its own, especially if we lack needed support. If those feelings of "brokenness" and its impact on others are what lead you to seek help, there is no shame in that, either. If anything, it speaks to your big, caring heart. Once that heart can learn to better prioritize its own needs—prioritize *you*, first and foremost—a tremendous amount of growth and healing can unfold.

Another possible scenario involves a partner or other loved one fueling your *I am such a problem* feelings. Perhaps your own trauma and the ways it manifests are fueling the flame of a partner's wounds. Samantha, for example, was triggered by certain types of kink play when she fell in love with Clarise, who cherishes those very practices. And Clarise interpreted Samantha's discomfort and attempts at boundary-setting as rejection, which Clarise endured to profound degrees by her parents during her childhood. Once they realized they were triggering each other, they sought couples therapy and ended up finding mutual healing after several months of supported effort.

In these cases, if you're both willing to do the work, you might both end up growing as individuals while your relationship strengthens too. "I can't say I'm exactly thrilled we had those effects on each other," Samantha said, "but now that we're in a better place, I can say it's all for sure been worth it." Their relationship is stronger, she added, and, most important, they've both experienced levels of growth and healing they hadn't even known were possible. "The awareness alone was huge," Samantha said, "but we also needed to figure out practical steps we could take, like finding activities we can both enjoy and creating a space for [Clarise] to have the kind of play she was missing on her own that we both are comfortable with." The pair also found that listening to each other with the aim of understanding what felt painful or triggering and why made a positive difference. "Once we understood where we were both coming from, it's like we softened and we could just comfort and be there for each other during triggered times, versus fighting about it."

If a loved one is shaming you endlessly and refuses to support you or face their own anger, pain, or agitation, a trauma-focused relationship therapist can help you determine your next best steps—whether that means reparative efforts through setting firm boundaries, seeking individual therapy for you both, or distancing yourself from or ending that relationship when desired or necessary. Truly loving and supportive partners worth keeping in your life might struggle to support you in ideal ways, but they will have your best interests at heart. When that's true, any growth and healing you collectively commit to are possible with appropriate effort. If it's not true, and you decide to move forward without that particular relationship, similar growth and healing are possible for your own life. In either case, you are worthy.

Unhelpful comments a partner might say (before knowing and doing better) include:

"Stop crying!"

"You never want sex."

"At some point, you're going to have to just get over it."

"How am I supposed to function when you're like this?"

"It's been weeks/months/years, and you're STILL upset?"

"You just want attention."

In many cases, these comments and misunderstandings involve socialization they may not even be aware of, especially in the case of straight, cisgender men, who often learn that "being emotional" is a weakness and men should be able to "fix everything" for women. They may have the best of intentions and love you with all of their hearts. But like you, they have a rich amount of learning, unlearning, and healing to do. Once they learn that there are physiological, neurological reasons for feeling triggered or activated, they'll hopefully be able to foster compassion and greater support for you, once they grow aware of effective steps. Also similar to your journey, this unpacking of beliefs and shifts in behaviors can lead to betterment in many life areas.

THE IMPACT ON PLEASURE

Feeling like we're a problem can function as a block from pleasure, for understandable reasons. Seeking pleasure requires at least some amount of believing that we're worthy of it. Why do something so "indulgent" when (we believe) we're a bothersome wreck? It's not uncommon to shut down more and more while dealing with trigger flares, spending more time on work or other obligations that feel doable while our own pleasure falls to the wayside. It's as though a light inside us is being overshadowed, so much so that we can forget that the light exists to begin with.

And pleasure requires reaching, extending outward to bring something close. When we feel problematic, it's like being tightly clenched and unable to expend the energy required to make that effort. But even if you don't feel worthy of pleasure, you can cultivate it in your life—as long as you believe you're allowed to do so. Let this be your permission slip.

you are allowed to seek joy and enjoy pleasure

TEN COMMON PLEASURE TRAPS

Many factors can lead us to fall into pleasure traps, or patterns of choices and behaviors that prevent or reduce our ability to truly step into and embrace pleasure or gain the many benefits pleasure can bring—particularly while we're managing trauma. Chiefly among these factors are harmful societal messages we've absorbed and that we tend to pass down from generation to generation. If you relate to the following traps, practice self-compassion. It's not your fault that you bear witness to pervasive messaging that brings harm. Gaining awareness of these types of scenarios can enable us to challenge them. In doing so, bit by bit, we can better our respective lives and the society we live in.

1. Sex with a partner feels too intense or triggering, so you avoid sexual (or sensual) pleasure altogether.

2. You find yourself pleasure-procrastinating. When it comes time to engage in something pleasurable, cleaning the house, running an errand, or other tasks suddenly seem urgent.

3. You would find pleasure in a particular activity with a partner, but it's not their favorite. So you opt to deny yourself that pleasure. "Why would I do something just for me?"

4. Seeking pleasure would require help or a particular sexual or sensual pursuit, and you don't allow yourself to discover how or where to seek it.

5. You've felt judged by others for embracing a particular type of pleasure, and in response, you shy away from it.

6. You consider yourself too old, wrinkled, thin, fat, curvy, small-breasted, small-penised, or *fill-in-the-blank* to engage in a pleasurable activity, such as sex or wearing a fitted swimsuit, so you cover up and attempt to stifle your desires instead.

7. You believe that indulging in a type of pleasure, such as eating decadent food you desire or satisfying a fantasy or fetish, would make you weak, so you choose self-denial over freedom.

8. You deny yourself pleasure because you haven't met a particular goal or standard, and therefore attempt to punish yourself with restriction. "I haven't earned it yet."

9. You fear that if you delight in "too much" pleasure, you'll never be able to stop, becoming a "lazy" or "gluttonous" person, so you avoid it altogether.

10. Communicating with a partner or loved one about your desires feels intimidating, so you stay silent and attempt to forget about them instead.

Journaling Prompt

Which of the above traps, if any, do you relate to? Describe a time when you've fallen into one of these traps, offer yourself care and compassion, then consider another option for the future. What steps could you take to better prioritize pleasure, given the chance? How might your life feel different if you didn't feel pulled into these traps, and instead stepped further into pleasure?

RENÉ: ADHD AND SELF-UNDERSTANDING

René Brooks was first diagnosed with attention deficit hyperactivity disorder at age seven, after a teacher had her tested without her mother's permission. Someone at the school essentially told her mom, "Hey, your kid has ADHD. Go get that taken care of," René recalled, to which her mother replied, "There's nothing wrong with my kid." René wasn't told about the diagnosis, only that the school had wanted her to take medication. Finally, at age twenty-five, René learned that ADHD, a treatable condition, underlaid so many of her often debilitating symptoms.

"I was on my therapist's couch getting treated for depression and I was like, 'Oh yeah, they tried to medicate me [for ADHD] when I was a kid,'" René said. "She cut me off mid-sentence . . . and said, 'I want you to go down the hallway and meet with my colleague. He's an ADHD specialist . . . and when you're done with that, we'll resume here. There's nothing even for us to talk about until we figure out this part.'"

Soon, it all made sense to René, why although she was a gifted child, she perpetually heard that she wasn't trying hard enough or fulfilling her potential. "You don't want people to be frustrated with you, but I couldn't do what was being asked of me," she said. "There's a trauma in knowing that you're doing every single thing that you can and it's still not good enough. And you're being told that you're not even trying, even though you are pulling out all the stops. Like, 'Why can't you get it together?' That was a part of my identity for a long time."

Into adulthood and before the diagnosis that stuck, René struggled in virtually every area of her life. Like many people with ADHD, she couldn't choose where she placed her focus, and grappled with forgetfulness, rejection sensitivity, and impulsivity that fueled poor choices. "Then you're picking bad relationships and you're making bad financial decisions," she added, noting that her car was towed repeatedly. And at one point she bounced checks so frequently the fees swallowed up an entire paycheck. René also endured an abusive romantic domestic relationship, which seems to occur at a higher rate in people with ADHD, likely because of abusers' tendency to prey on people's vulnerability. People with ADHD tend to be highly empathetic too, and wish to help others, even—or especially, René believes—when they struggle to help themselves. "All of these things continually bring trauma into your life," René said. "I was a hot mess."

René is far from alone in how difficult that ongoing ordeal became. Many experts believe that ADHD raises one's risk for trauma for a variety of reasons, from being bullied because of your differences to having chronically low self-esteem in spheres that aren't designed terribly well for neurodivergent brains. Many people who have ADHD believe that a lack of diagnosis and treatment—which is more common among women, femmes, and people of color—can be a source of trauma in itself. In July 2020, August posted a poll in an online support group for people with ADHD that asked, "Do you consider undiagnosed/untreated ADHD a source of trauma?," over 70 percent of the more than two hundred people who responded said, "Yes, definitely." Only four people checked the option for "No, not really." The remaining answers involved some rendition of "it depends," based on factors such as parenting and symptom severity.

People with ADHD who remain undiagnosed or lack access to treatment hold heightened risks for potentially dangerous complications, such as an inability to hold down a job, alcohol dependency, severe anxiety and depression, car accidents, and even death. Psychologist Russell Barkley, who believes his twin brother, Ron, died in an accident due to ADHD, conducted research on the life-threatening impact of the disorder. His study showed that severe ADHD can shorten a person's life by twenty-five years, and "irreparable harm can befall adults with ADHD when on the road," and "those with driving problems can be helped by medication." For these reasons, René doesn't buy into the relatively common notion that ADHD is a gift. "I think it nullifies and dismisses experiences like that," she said. "And when you think of something as a gift, you're not looking for the danger." That's not to say that the ADHD brain, like all brains, doesn't have its strengths. As Edward Hallowell, MD, who has and treats ADHD, said in an interview for the *ADHD Experts Podcast*, "If you have ADHD, you have a Ferrari for a brain. . . . The problem is, you have bicycle brakes. If you build up the brakes, you can change the world for the better." Focusing on your strengths, getting needed support, and self-understanding can go far.

Thankfully, once she was properly diagnosed, René's job provided health insurance that covered helpful medication. Due to her income she's also able to cover co-pays, which for some can be cost-prohibitive. And since starting treatment, her life has completely changed. She's far better organized, nurtures a healthy relationship with her husband, enjoys higher self-esteem, and can be more intentional about pleasure. She also launched a career that supports others in the ADHD community. A few years ago, she founded *Black Girl, Lost Keys*, a blog that empowers Black women with ADHD and teaches them to better thrive. "What the internet doesn't know is that I'm also an award-winning poet and I've won awards for short stories," she said. "I'm actually a writer who just so happens to blog. . . . And I feel like if you have the skill and you have the access, you have a responsibility to help."

René also provides ADHD coaching, a form of support she has benefited from personally. And once she was able to get a handle on her ADHD, she felt ready to partake in trauma therapy. "Therapy helps you process trauma and depression that so often coincide with or stem from ADHD," she said, "and coaching helps you achieve goals in the present tense." And just as trauma-focused therapy is important when you're addressing the effects of trauma, choosing ADHD-specific coaching over general support is crucial because neurodivergent minds function so differently. Otherwise, feeling misunderstood and being instructed in ways that won't help can feel frustrating or even traumatizing, especially if you spent too long not understanding your needs, challenges, or ways of functioning. "Going to trauma therapy was what really helped me to sort out a lot of my history [with untreated ADHD] and it's changed the way that I evaluate the relationships that I allow in my life," she said. "I think everyone with ADHD should have trauma therapy."

As René has grown and cultivated deeper self-understanding and acceptance, she's also distanced herself from damaging friendships. "I feel like this is a common ADHD experience too," she said. "When you are the jacked-up friend for so long, people get used to you being the jacked-up friend and they like you that way because they have some-one to throw their shit on. . . . So I had quite a few friends who were like, 'She's not a hot mess anymore. Now we need to find a new way to kind of put her down,' or they didn't know how to interact with me when I wasn't 'crazy.'" Connecting with fellow neurodivergent folks had the opposite effect, bringing a sense of community and validation she hadn't before experienced. "I can remember the first ADHD group I ever joined on Facebook," she said. "I would be scrolling and I would be talking to my then husband like, 'Look! No, look at this!' It's *me*."

In full circle fashion, René's mother, the woman who was told her daughter needed medication, yet wasn't provided any resources or con-text for understanding two decades ago, was recently diagnosed with ADHD herself. "People hear that and tell me it's so inspirational, that I led her to that, but no. It wasn't me," René said with a laugh. "She figured it out from listening to a podcast." At the same time, her mom did witness René's struggles over the years, plus a decade of healing and renewal she's embraced since her ADHD has been managed. All of that has surely played important roles in her mother's journey.

Every now and then, René looks back on her earlier life and won-ders if all of the experiences she recalls actually happened, given how dramatic many were. That ADHD tends to create nonlinear mem-ories and fuel self-doubt, especially when diagnosis is delayed, can make such things even more difficult to sort out. "So every once in a while, I'll call someone and go, 'I'm not making this shit up, right?

Like this really did happen like this, didn't it?' And they're like, 'Yeah, of course it did. Remember when XYZ happened?' and I'm like, 'OK, cool. I didn't think that I was imagining it this way, but just in case, I just needed some confirmation there. Thank you.'" Being better able to seek support in this way is one of countless rewards René has gained through support and self-understanding, attributes she continues to shed light on and encourage in the neurodivergent community. To folks in that community who continue to feel alone or stuck, or unable to afford proper care potentially *because* of issues related to ADHD, she said, "Maybe you can't afford therapy, but you might be able to find yourself a support group that can at least help you keep chugging along . . . for almost like little boosts, until you get to the point where you can do something more. There's no one who has ADHD who should not be interacting with neurodiverse people on a regular basis. If for nothing else, the opportunity to feel normal is something that everyone should be able to have. And that's what we do for each other every time we log on and talk about our experiences. It really takes you from feeling like you are damaged goods to going, 'Oh, this happens to other people too.'"

ROBERT AND HANNAH: BUILDING TRUST, INTIMACY, AND COMMUNICATION

Robert and Hannah met when they had both made good headway in their respective healing journeys. Robert was well into his dedicated year off from dating and sex to focus on healing following an abusive relationship. Hannah already had a crush on the "idea of him," having been told by a mutual friend how good, kind, and respectful he was, when Hannah and Robert connected at a Thanksgiving gathering.

Robert and a friend organized the holiday get-together for people who were estranged from their relatives because of reasons such as abuse, something both he and Hannah knew well.

Hannah had endured years of emotional incest by her father, her primary abuser, who regularly made inappropriate comments and took sexualized photos of her. She and her mother also believe that he sexually abused her when she was quite small. Robert, too, endured significant abuse throughout his youth, including beatings by his father, verbal abuse by both of his parents, and sexual assault by men, first at age ten and again during college. Both recovering alcoholics who had been deeply engaged in self-work, Hannah's and Robert's paths crossed and then merged at seemingly an ideal time. While neither of them believe that you have to be "healed" or "fully love yourself" to find love, they're grateful to have met at a time when they weren't in the rawest of states and felt ready to consider building a healthy, lasting intimate relationship. That was decades, a wedding, and two children ago.

Hannah reached a positive turning point in her early twenties, when she was finally able to name the abuse she had endured. "I described what had happened at my last visit with him to the therapist that I was seeing at the time," she said. "She was like, 'Do you know that that's incest?' And I'm like, 'No, but that really explains a lot of things.' And it was really amazing to me because . . . my entire life up until that point, I just thought I was completely insane and that I probably wasn't interpreting the world accurately. It was the piece that allowed me to really start healing."

Robert also found healing through work with a therapist and twelve-step meetings as well as reading *The Courage to Heal* by Ellen

Bass and Harriet Lerner's *The Dance of Anger*. And both Hannah and Robert continue to find strength and restoration through their relationship based on trust and mutual respect. From the beginning, they've committed to moving along slowly, with every step from having sex for the first time to having children. Meanwhile, they've both struggled with fears that they will somehow "mess [their children] up."

Prior to having kids, when Hannah worked as a nanny for various families, she started to see that there are different ways to parent, beyond the abusive tactics she grew up with. She also faced fears that many incest survivors endure: that they'll be triggered into abusing children as well, or that doing so is somehow engrained in them. "I had to spend a lot of time talking with my therapist about the difference between noticing that people have bodies and actually being sexually aroused by that and/or acting on that arousal, and that those are all very different things," she said. "From the start, I had no concept of the difference between noticing that the baby I was changing had a penis and being an abuser."

Robert has faced similar challenges. "I always let the woman take the lead [with sex], because I had a lot of fear because of my early sexual experiences," he said. "I was afraid I was going to turn into an abuser." And as thrilled as he is to be raising daughters, he has also worried that something would shift and he would start feeling sexual attraction toward them. "That's never happened, but the anxiety is there," he noted. Recognizing that the anxiety exists and why, he said, has helped him and Hannah navigate these emotions without feeling overwhelmed by them. Meanwhile, they remain committed to raising their girls to be empowered in their bodies and sexuality, in ways neither of them had the chance to early on. They never shame their daughters for dressing as they wish, for example, or place value in their looks. They encourage sex-positivity by allowing for curiosities and questions around sex, rather than shaming or silencing them, and modeling boundaries and communication in all aspects of their lives.

These practices take high priority in the bedroom too. Each time Robert and Hannah have sex, they communicate what specifics they'll engage in in advance. Because Hannah still struggles to readily embrace pleasure, they take plenty of time for her to get into a relaxed mindset. They'll often start their intimate time together by listening to an NPR puzzle podcast or playing a nonsexual game. For Hannah, conversation and other forms of intellectual stimulation seem to pave the way for arousal.

Now that their bodies are changing with middle age and menopause, they apply the same communication and adaptation skills they've developed over the years to embrace the different ways their bodies respond. And in some ways, their sex life has grown more vibrant over time. "It's actually easier for me to have fun with sex now that the kids are older," Hannah said. When the children were small, she said, shifting from parenting mode to being lovers, when they finally had enough time and privacy, felt especially challenging because of her abuse history. And while they have both felt triggered by other people's touch, Hannah has found that she enjoys a good foot massage, so Robert purchased a book to study up on giving her a great one. Finding such ways to delight in pleasure that feel comfortable and prioritizing open communication at every step continues to enhance their lives and their relationship while chipping away at the negative effects of the traumas they endured early on. These efforts aren't easy or cure-alls, they agree, but they're profoundly helpful and worthwhile.

August: One thing that struck me about René, Robert, and Hannah's stories was how impactful finding therapists who were a good fit for them was. I love that René saw a therapist specifically for trauma and then worked with an ADHD coach, and how important both can be for neurodivergent folks.

Jamila: Mmm, yes. The beginnings of René's story were so painful. I feel like there was such significant ableism and racism in the school not really informing the mother of the context, just that your kid needs to have this. And I can imagine she's busy. There's a lot going on in her life. There's a common message of "you're probably not a good mom, Black woman, so we're going to tell you how you should be better." I can imagine her feeling confused and scared and angry. And so for me, the systemic disregard and racism is very strong there. And then René finding her way over time, going through significant stuff, and then reaching out for the therapy and coaching. It's almost like, "There's scar tissue, but there's also nothing inherently wrong with me. I just need support around my differences." That was triumphant.

August: Absolutely. And now she's paying it all forward so beautifully in her work. And Robert and Hannah are raising autonomous, empowered daughters. I love that they had their own respective therapists, which seemed to play a big role in their ability to move forward in their lives and also cultivate a healthy relationship together.

Jamila: The fact that Robert and Hannah had done their own work and sought support for some years before finding each other, and had really committed to *I want to be better*, and then met each other quasi-randomly, but within their shared community, is wonderful. That's what I want for most people, to do whatever healing work you can do and then bring that healing into relationships. That doesn't mean that there's not more to be done, but that you'll have self-awareness, insight, and tools that will then be even more useful as you're building an intimate relationship. That's so beautiful. For Robert and Hannah, that didn't mean that they didn't struggle once they were together, but they're able to be creative and understand that the other person was not the problem. Often in couples, when there's trauma, it can feel as though *you're the problem* or *I'm the problem*. And instead, it seems like they were both like, *No, we have challenges and we can figure it out*.

August: When someone is struggling—trauma is interfering with their life and they want to start therapy and invite those relationship benefits as well—what is a good first step?

Jamila: It's often an exhausting and emotionally draining process, right? Where do you go? And how do you go about it while you're in the midst of every other day or every day feeling awful? My answer is to slow it down. Write down what your symptoms are, what's causing the most distress: "I can't sleep" or "I'm fighting all the time" or "I'm harming myself." Make a short list. And then, when you're ready to start looking for a therapist, set a time limit or only look into, say, three people that day. Take supersmall steps. Trauma can be overwhelming, so ask friends or even a trusted acquaintance for specific help, "Can you help me with this?" or "Can I call you just to check in or text you?" I would say don't do it alone.

August: I love that. It never even occurred to me when I was looking for a therapist to ask someone to help. What a load off, to know that you aren't carrying that labor by yourself. Even if you're fortunate enough to be able to go through insurance, they might give you a list of ten or more people. Without insurance, you may need to find someone with a sliding scale or other lower-cost options. And regardless, you have to deal with schedules and perhaps having to ask questions or share information that may feel vulnerable or difficult.

Jamila: Yes. Asking someone, "Can you just sit with me?" or "Can I talk to you afterward?" Or, "Hey, I'm gonna make the calls at this time." If I could go back in my own process . . . the first time, when I was looking for support while I was in so much pain, I wish I had known I could ask somebody.

August: Another thing I love about that is the accountability piece. For me, when I felt like I knocked on five doors and nothing worked out, it was easy to give up. I gave up several times and then thought, "Oh, I'll be OK." And then I'd be triggered again and think, *Why didn't I keep trying?* So to have someone gently follow up and cheer you on seems big.

Jamila: Yes. It's super important!

August: What about making sure a therapist is a good fit for you? Once you finally have an appointment, you might have really high hopes that it'll work out well. And if not, do you want to go through that labor again? I know I've gone into therapy thinking, *I know it's* *supposed to be hard.* So sometimes red flags can seem like, *Oh, maybe that's just me having to work through this.* What can we look out for, especially at that first appointment?

Jamila: Basically, what you're looking for is does this person seem organized? And that they're really wanting to listen. In the middle of trauma, what we need is flexible and empathic structure. I almost walked away from some of the best work I ever did with a therapist because I thought she was too nice. So that might happen sometimes with trauma, where we've been surviving with such harshness and we're like, *I need to get out of this. I need somebody to be tough with me and call me on my shit,* and that's actually not what we need. If the person seems pleasant and caring, that's probably a good sign. Conversely, if they seem rigid or unable to answer questions—particularly when people have certain ethnicity, gender, sexual orientation, or class pieces coming up—don't go any further. You don't want the nightmares of going weeks, months, or even years while feeling trapped with the wrong therapist.

August: Right, because when we're feeling triggered or going through trauma, we probably already feel trapped. We didn't choose it, and we're trying to feel more free, not less. So that seems like the last thing we'd need.

Jamila: Yes. And if you call someone new you'd like to work with and they don't call you back in a few days, go ahead and try again. But no more than around two follow-ups. Another major red flag is if they talk about themselves a lot or have kind of built-in assumptions. For all of my first sessions, I say, "Take a couple of days to think about how the session went for you." And if I want to work with them, I'll say, "I would like to work with you. Take a couple of days and then let me know if you want to make another appointment." But some therapists will say at the end of the session, "Do you want to make another appointment?" And if we're dealing with trauma, being put on the spot does not feel good.

August: That sort of pressure can bring up so many things: *I don't want to be mean*, or *Maybe they know best*, or *I don't have a choice.*

Jamila: Right. For me, every single step of the process with a client is letting them know that they can slow down, ask questions, and collaborate with me. And even if they don't take me up on any of that, I try to create a structure where all of this is a choice. If there's a feeling that you can freely express your wants or needs, that's really great.

August: I don't think everyone realizes that not all therapists specialize in trauma. What would you say about seeking someone who specifically lists trauma with their credentials?

Jamila: To be very blunt, if a therapist is not listing trauma informed, somatics, interpersonal neurobiology, mind/body work, mindfulness, or other modalities that support social justice and trauma management in their specialties, look elsewhere. Most of us are carrying some kind of trauma, acute or chronic, just given the statistics around assaults on LGBTQ folks, femmes, women, which we know are underreported, and assaults for men, which are, of course, severely underreported, as well as economic stress, issues around race . . .

If the therapist is not trauma informed, I do not believe the therapy is going to be that effective. Trauma-informed care is based on how the body and relationships actually work, which is that wellness and sustainable progress occur when there is enough emotional and physical support to withstand the inter- and intrapersonal storms that are going to happen. You can, however, adapt any theoretical modality and make it relational and trauma-informed. You can do CBT in a relational way, absolutely. But if that awareness, transparency, safety, rapport, collaboration and co-regulation is not there, then I think it will disempower the client and frustrate the therapist. So I highly recommend that people look for care providers who practice from this framework.

August: Oh, that's so big. It brought to mind another piece that I've thought about quite a bit. . . . I know there's a lot of overlap with depression and anxiety and trauma, and with neurodivergence and trauma. Or maybe it's important for you to find someone who shares your gender or race or value system. Beyond looking for someone who's trauma-informed, are there other things that people should be aware of or look for, based on their own unique needs?

Jamila: One thing that people don't always know is possible—and with insurance companies being what they are, it's not always possible—but you can go to your insurance company and say, "You don't have anybody who fits what I'm looking for. I found somebody and I want them included." And then you go as high up the organizational ladder as you can. Don't necessarily even talk to the first person you reach. Go as far up the ladder as you can and say, "I want this therapist to have a single case agreement with you or for the therapist to be an out-of-network provider and for me to be reimbursed, because I've been through your network and you don't have what I need."

I definitely encourage people to try to find somebody who really can hit all the boxes. And that being said, sometimes it's just not possible. And so it becomes a matter of like, "OK, what is it that I'm really needing the most? And what can I be flexible about?" For some clients, like people of color that I've worked with or who wanted to work with me, they say, "I have to be able to sit across from a person who looks like me. That's the most important thing." And if needed, I may say, "Hey, I'm not available, but here are a small number of people that I trust who have expertise that pertains to these other pieces that you're looking at." That again goes back to that first conversation with a therapist. Can they make room for that? And to me, a fifteen-to-twenty-minute consultation conversation with a potential therapist is not unreasonable.

August: When you're working with clients, how often do you hear "I am a problem"? Whether they say it flat out or you can just tell that's how they feel.

Jamila: I couldn't put a percentage on it, but most of the time there's this sense that "I'm uncontrollable" or "I'm broken" or "I should be handling this better. I am hurting my partner. And I don't know why or I just don't want them around me." There's just a lot of internalizing of blame and responsibility and sometimes it's like, "I should be better." But other times it's this oversized responsibility like, "I wish that I wanted sex more so my partner would be satisfied" or that "I wish I didn't have these 'strange' reactions. I know I'm confusing or upsetting my partner and the people around me." So it's very painful. Those feelings are normal when we're trying to recover from trauma. We blame ourselves.

August: That's really a comforting thought because I feel like it can become a cycle of shaming ourselves for feeling like we're a problem. Then *that* can become another trauma.

Jamila: I completely agree and it becomes this sad catch-22 or layers of the original trauma, which one obviously didn't have support around, and then the blaming of oneself, and then the sense that "I can't get out of this" and then "what's wrong with me?"—and it becomes multiple levels. You are in this painful cycle.

August: I imagine it could also be the reason people seek help. Because trauma can affect our self-worth, it's sometimes easier to get help when you want to be a "better partner," and when you're not quite in a place of, "I want to feel happier. I want to feel more peaceful. I want to have better sleep" or wanting that goodness for yourself. Could these feelings provide a helpful catalyst of sorts, if they get someone through the door and on the path of "I need help?"

Jamila: Yes, I definitely see that where clients will say, "My anger, my not wanting to have sex or sex is painful for me or I push them away, so I need to be here and can you fix this so that I can be a good partner?" And I don't think that that's a bad impetus to come in. One of my deepest beliefs is that at its core, relationship is necessary and nourishing. We do things for others that sometimes we aren't able to do for ourselves. And I think that's something that should be valued and supported. So if that's the reason that somebody comes in to see me I'm like, "Cool, OK." And what I'm conceptualizing is, "How do I help them understand what's happening? How do I build in some supports, so they can let their partner know what's happening, let their partner know what's occurring?" I do like to work with the other partner(s) or loved ones, friends, or confidants of my clients. I get consent from the client and extend an invitation to them that if at any time they want their partner to come in, their partner is more than welcome so I can share with them some information about trauma and how it impacts us. This way it's not just one person holding all this information, because how else are they supposed to be supported? It's like this little plant that's trying to grow on its own. If the little plant doesn't have enough support and nutrients, how is it going to thrive?

For more on seeking support and getting started with therapy, see chapter 4.

Grounding Exercise

Seated stamping. Sit on a chair and tap or stamp your left foot into the ground, then do the same with your right foot. Repeat this process for a while—left foot, right foot, left foot, right foot—finding a pace that feels soothing to you. For added relaxation, give yourself a gentle hug while you tap or stamp, placing each hand on your opposite forearm.

6

"Healing Is Taking Too Long."

Imagine you're strolling along on a quiet beach beside the ocean. Ahead of you the coastline seems to stretch on and on forever with shifting sandy landscapes on one side of you and the expanse of the ocean on the other. As you glance ahead, do you think you'd be worried about getting to the end of the beach? Or wondering why the heck doing so is taking so long? Probably not. More likely, you would notice the fresh, misty air on your skin, the powdery or pebbly sand shifting below your feet, the sound of birds chirping in the distance. If it's a hot day, you might pause for a refreshing dip in the water or to apply more sunscreen, or aloe vera, if you'd already experienced some burn. Regardless of the specifics, the slower you go, the more you'll fully experience and benefit from the wondrous parts or any challenges that occur. Managing trauma works similarly. We're not suggesting that with a simple mindset shift you can turn it into a day at the beach. What we do want for you is to trust that goodness and rewards aren't merely at the journey's end, but within your reach throughout. And that the slower you allow yourself to move forward, the further you'll go in your healing and into your pleasure.

There's no denying it. Managing trauma can feel downright grueling at times. It doesn't, however, have to be grueling all of the time. Chances are you'll have moments, hours, days, or even weeks when it feels as though the healing process is too much to bear (the "sun" is too hot), and as though the time and energy it requires is black-hole vast. You have every right to those feelings; they are valid. *You* are valid. It's important to note, though, that those feelings need not be permanent.

All throughout your healing journey, there will be easier times, which will strike a noticeable contrast to the rockier periods. You might not even think about the time passage when the bright spots happen. Sometimes by intentionally focusing on such times—the happier parts, the pleasure—we're better able to navigate the lows. And as difficult as it can seem, giving ourselves full permission to heal as long as we need to can account for some of the most important work we ever do. Some folks consider healing lifelong, which isn't necessarily negative, but can instead be seen as a perpetual commitment to unlearning, new learning, and a lifetime of blossoming.

The same philosophies apply to sex and intimate relationship challenges when you're managing trauma. Many people seek out the "right" tips or tricks to get their sex life back on track, hoping for a quick fix. In reality, there is no hack that can improve sex or intimacy—no sex toy, special position, or spicy date night. While all of these tools can play a role and bring valuable benefits, they cannot substitute for slowing down and paying attention to the experience you and your partner(s) are having. There is no accelerant a sex therapist can give you. The slower you go, the more likely you'll be to experience deeper pleasure and orgasm(s) and feel more connected to your partner(s). As with emotional healing from trauma, sexual healing and related brain changes emerge when you allow for time, space, and presence.

Slowing down is important when you feel triggered too. Taking deep breaths and aiming to accept what's happening ("I am feeling triggered and I won't feel this way forever," versus fighting with all of your might: "I must stop this!") can help reduce the strain during the flare-up and allow it to pass more quickly. In this way, you can see it as a wave (or tsunami) that's taking you under. But if you relax as much as is possible, you will surface. Another way to think about it is that it's similar to a menopausal hot flash. Many people who experience these bouts of intense body heat and perspiration find that knowing they will last about X number of minutes helps ease the get-me-out-of-my-skin frustration. We can deal with almost anything for a limited time. Reminding ourselves of this and viewing each activated time as an opportunity to practice supreme self-care, in whatever ways we may need, can turn it into challenging, yet restorative, time. And the benefits of that practice will carry on well into the future.

NATALIE: AWARENESS, REFRAMING, AND ORGASMIC MEDITATION

Like many folks, Natalie Hatjes, MS, CHT, didn't realize that she'd been learning to manage trauma and seek healing until years in. Her experiences with trauma started when she was molested during child-hood, an event she doesn't remember, and worsened with an abusive relationship in adulthood.

"I think it was maybe eight years that I was feeling very just checked out with myself," she said. "I thought I was strong and could do everything on my own, and 'no, of course this isn't bothering me.'" One night at a networking event she attended, in hopes of making connections in the new area she'd moved to, she was invited to a med-itation class by its leader, a healing practitioner. After participating in the class, Natalie slept well for the first time in as long as she could remember. She then had an energy healing massage from the woman and began really focusing on loving and caring for herself.

"Throughout that process, I healed, and I don't even think that I was doing it intentionally," she recalled, describing healing as a by-product of the journey back to loving herself. One reason Natalie wasn't aware that she needed healing earlier on stemmed from the fact that the perpetrator of some of her biggest traumas—rape, abuse, and assault—was her then intimate partner. "Especially at the time, I didn't realize it was rape," she noted. "I didn't realize I was being abused and assaulted because he was my boyfriend. I had that opinion myself."

She wrote a poem about the experience entitled, "I Was Raped . . . by My Boyfriend." The ellipses represent the hesitation and difficulty people often have in believing that sexual assault often happens at the hands of loved ones, not strangers, even though statistics show that nearly twenty people per minute are physically abused by an intimate partner in the United States alone.

Natalie now works as a sex coach and hypnotherapist and helps people manage triggers related to trauma, guiding them toward greater self-awareness and self-compassion so they can learn to react differently when triggers arise. An example she recalls from her own life involves the sound of a key in her door. "After I moved to Florida, a guy that I was dating was in town. And he said, 'I'm going to go down to the bar for a little bit. I'm going to come back in a couple hours.' Well, he had my key and I was in bed. I was either asleep or almost asleep and I heard the key in the door and it automatically made me very scared and anxious and I could just feel it in my body. The key at the door and knowing that he had been at the bar was a huge trigger for me. But as soon as he came in, I reminded myself that he wasn't my ex-boyfriend. It was a different guy. I told myself, 'OK, I'm safe . . . I'm OK.'"

Natalie is grateful for the personal and professional work that has allowed her to reach a place where she can recognize and respect when these types of trigger flares are happening. In the past, she might have felt anxious for no apparent reason, she said, lashed out at her boyfriend, or started an argument to avoid having the sex she feared.

Recognizing a trigger episode as just that, as Natalie did, without shaming ourselves for experiencing it, may take time and practice. More than likely, it will. And even then, we may still feel triggered. Gradually, though, we may find that we're less activated, can experience relief much sooner, or feel less exhaustion afterward. Over time, trigger storms may even arise less often. And the care and grace we give ourselves will extend into every area of our lives.

There is no time limit on managing trauma or your learning curve surrounding it. If you have moments when it feels like healing is taking "forever" or as though you'll "always deal with this," remind yourself that *you are evolving*. You may have to deal with triggers for some time, or even indefinitely. *But you are growing.* Triggers will not always feel the same way, and healing is not linear. What you might consider a setback or relapse is likely part of the process. It's also completely normal.

A shift in life circumstances might bring about a spree of activated spurts after months, or even years, without such occurrences. You might feel more sensitive to triggers during particular times of years, on certain anniversaries, or, if you menstruate, at various points in your cycle.

All of this is common and not a cause for shame. Similarly, you might expect to feel more trigger-sensitive around certain people or events and then welcome the surprise of feeling calm and steady instead.

Regardless of how your path unfolds, you can delight in pleasure all along the way. Some days that pleasure may be as simple as wearing your comfiest, coziest clothes, taking time to sway in a rocking chair, or sipping a cup of tea. Other days, pleasure might stem from taking a needed shower, scheduling a therapy appointment, scheduling intimate time with a partner, or talking or laughing with a friend. The possibilities for pleasure are endless when we expand our definition of what it can entail and commit to prioritizing pleasure as a practice.

> Pleasure practices can become a rebellious "F-you" to trauma-based triggers and bolster your healing journey at the same time.

Natalie's life is now rich with pleasure of many kinds. One practice she recommends to clients and enjoys herself is orgasmic meditation. After growing up around a lot of religious shame related to masturbation, she now embraces solo play and sensual self-touch as wonderful ways to connect with and honor her body. "I do meditative touch and just follow my own lead, follow my body," she said about mindful masturbation. "Sometimes even with an orgasm, if you imagine it as an explosion or if you imagine it as something opening up, it's really like the release is releasing the shame and the guilt or whatever negative emotion that you have leaving with the orgasm."

Mindful Solo Play Exercise

Set aside time to be alone in an inviting space where you feel safe and comfortable. Choose an amount of time that feels doable and nourishing rather than stressful. For some people that may be five minutes. For others, fifteen, thirty, or more. Using items you have on hand, create a soothing atmosphere.

Place candles on your bedside table, for example, and pull out your favorite soft or satiny blanket. Think about all of your senses, enhancing your atmosphere with whatever seems enticing: sensual music or an erotic story to listen to, scented oils in a diffuser for aroma, a soft fan for a breeze on your skin, a lubricant or massage oil for added ease and arousal. When it's time to play, do what you can to relax your body. Take slow, deep breaths. Close your eyes, if that feels helpful.

Then explore your body, starting with any area of your skin that feels intimate or erogenous. Orgasm can be a part of this, and it's OK if that's one of your goals. It's not, however, by any means required. When you're finished, reflect on your experience, jotting your thoughts down in a journal or email to yourself or reading them into a voice memo.

You are worthy of pleasure.

Jamila's Reflections

When I'm beginning to work with my clients around trauma and pleasure, I introduce the concept of paradox. Paradox, the way I intend it, is about two things that seem as though they cannot possibly coexist but when we set them next to one another in our minds or bodies and allow them to both be true, they can illuminate a third way that gives us a path forward. For example, sometimes something can be exciting but scary at the same time. That doesn't mean we are lying to ourselves or that we have to only be excited or only be anxious, we can let ourselves experience the truth of both. When it comes to trauma, often people have been caught between what should have happened versus what did happen, or the feelings they had versus what they thought they were supposed to feel, horror where they expected to feel safe, fear where they hoped to feel comforted. This is not the same as saying everything is relative and there is no moral center—quite the opposite. The more we practice holding paradox as individuals and as a society, the more we might discover solutions to our seemingly unsolvable problems.

Beware the Binary

Years ago, this phrase came to Jamila as she was working with clients and noticing common themes: *beware of the binary.* If you've been through trauma or live in this society, it's easy to fall into this kind of thinking. American society prizes "good or bad," "right or wrong," "healthy or unhealthy," "thin or fat," "boy or girl," "gay or straight," and other binaries with rigid harshness. Value judgments based on these ideas cause harm. If you feel caught between these binaries, and therefore believe you're failing, consider this: What might happen if you recognize that the binaries themselves are the problem? Numerous Indigenous cultures have long embraced the idea of a "third gender." Many tribal communities, distanced from the pressures of Hollywood beauty standards, respect all body shapes and sizes, without sexualizing particular body parts, such as breasts. Binary thinking is learned, and it can be resisted and unlearned.

Can you think of an experience where you felt opposing feelings at the same time? Can you identify the sensations connected to those feelings? If so, spend some time journaling about the experience.

I've found that this idea of paradox helps people to tolerate, then become curious about, and ultimately have compassion for, their own seemingly incompatible truths. This way, a person doesn't have to deny or throw away aspects of themselves. They don't have to pretend that only one truth is acceptable. To explain further, a client may still feel love, affection, or care for someone who abused them. This is an uncomfortable truth that many survivors experience. American culture carries messages that put unbearable stresses on people. There are cultural narratives that a survivor has to either hate or seem to be unbothered by their abuser. I often have clients admit with shame that they still love the person who harmed them and that people have told them that they are codependent and need to move on and get over that. Additionally, I've heard from clients that they've been told,

"Don't let that person take up space in your head" or "Don't let it bother you."

Also, depending on our culture, religion, or where we live, we are not always able to or don't always want to make a complete cut from people and situations that have or are harming us. I work with my clients to first discover and then identify their feelings, their narratives, and the pieces of their experiences that seem at odds with one another. We then work to learn about and track their somatic experiences so that they come to understand literally how they feel, learn to notice and tend to their bodies, as well as reach for support.

Unfortunately, this inability or lack of desire to create needed space just compounds the trauma because the person is being urged to deny or amputate part of their experience, as they had to do during the original violation(s). But love or care, fear or rage, and other strong emotions cannot be turned off just because we will it so. And it hurts to try to stop loving someone when that is how a part of us feels. I've never found it helpful to indicate to my clients that they must stop feeling a certain way. Emotions and our relational attachments are not spigots we can simply turn off, even if sometimes we wish to. If we can make room for paradox, then we are offering ourselves an escape away from binary thinking toward a holistic experience.

On a societal level, when marginalized people are expected to "just keep going" or told that they are "so strong," this reinforces the fragmentation of their experience and signals that there is no place to grieve, no possibility for safety or rest. Someone who is strong needs to rest to restore their strength. When we are hurt we must tend to the wound. And the greater the hurt, the more support that is needed.

BETH: INTERGENERATIONAL TRAUMA AND ANCESTRAL STRENGTH

Given the high rate of trauma and particularly sexual trauma among Indigenous populations, a climate of trauma was part of Beth's "normal" during childhood. While she didn't recognize that at the time, she said it all makes perfect sense in hindsight. Because of her mother's drug addiction, Beth was removed from that single-parent home early on and raised by her grandparents. By the time she reached kindergarten, her grandmother, the matriarch of her Diné (also known by the federally recognized name, Navajo) family, was teaching her to protect herself from a broad range of dangers. "If anyone ever touches you, this is how you move their hand away. Or if anyone tries to coerce you into something you don't want, you speak up . . . you let me know," she recalls learning. "And I was like, why is she always telling us this stuff? She was constantly reminding us of ways that we need to speak up, even at the doctor's office."

Years later, Beth realized that many of those warnings derived from her grandmother's own experience, including being assaulted by a physician as a child. Her grandmother also taught her how to physically fight and roll away from a moving car, should she be abducted, at an early age. All of this led Beth to feel empowered, in many ways—more aware than afraid. She knew what to do in "stranger-danger" situations and what to look out for from professionals she should be able to trust. Then something happened that she wasn't equipped for: being molested by a close family friend when she wasn't yet out of grade school. "I was prepared for someone trying to throw me in a corner . . . and how to tuck and roll [out of a car]," she said. "I had all these different strategies. This was so different than what I had imagined an assault would be on my body. And so I froze."

Soon after, she told one of her aunts about the assault. Rather than believe and support Beth, her aunt minimized it, saying she had probably just dreamed it. So Beth attempted to carry on while keeping a distance from the man at gatherings. A few years later, she started acting out at school. She used the fighting tactics she had learned to protect herself against others, particularly boys who bullied or took advantage of other kids.

"I was so frustrated and agitated," she said of her emotional state at the time, adding that the unaddressed trauma turned her into a "troubled middle schooler." As her behavioral track record worsened, a school counselor placed her in a support group for frequently disciplined teens. One day during a session, two of her peers shared that they had been molested. Feeling eager to "get it out" too, Beth spoke about her own assault. Then her cousin, also a member of the group, shared that she had been molested by the same person. Desperate to prevent further harm by this man, Beth and her cousin decided to file a report.

"I felt sad that my cousin and friends in that group had experienced some form of sexual abuse . . . but also a sense of like, OK, we have this shared experience. I'm not alone," Beth said, noting that before then, a sense of aloneness fostered shame. "And although it sucks to be saying this happened to all of us . . . I didn't feel so ashamed anymore. It just felt empowering." After Beth and her cousin filed a report, the man admitted to additional abuse he imposed on other girls, including members of his family, and he was sent to prison where he would stay for several years.

Thankfully, members of her family supported Beth and her cousin throughout all of this, including her mother, who was in jail herself at the time for drug charges. "Even though she wasn't physically around. . . she reminded me that I did the right thing by speaking up and said she was sorry that she wasn't able to protect me more," Beth said. "It was just nice to hear. I never got the like, 'Why didn't you say something before?' or 'It was your fault.'" Her grandmother continued to stay staunchly by her side, letting people know, before and after the abuser was released, that he was no longer welcome.

"She made it very clear to the family to exile this person from our family's lives," Beth said. "And I remember photos he was literally cut out of. There was this message, 'you don't have to see this person, even in a picture.'" Trauma from the assault affected Beth and her relationship to sex and pleasure in numerous ways. She wonders if the fact that she was sexually active at an early age, by twelve or thirteen, stems from the abuse. Regardless, she's grateful that her first experiences having sex were pleasurable and wanted equally by herself and her partners.

After high school, the effects of trauma grew more pronounced, she said, because rather than engaging in sex for fun, she was cultivating intimate relationships. Everything felt more serious and more sensual. The expectation to be affectionate, which she struggled to feel safe in, much less enjoy, felt like uncomfortable pressure. Soft touch felt foreign and triggering and when a partner would brush her leg gently or caress her to "get in the mood," she felt the urge to "just get to the point." Anything slow that involved gradually moving toward her pants reminded her of the assault. So for a while, Beth either avoided sex or took the dominant role. "I was like, 'I'm in control here,'" she recalled. "I'm gonna tell you what you're going to do and how you're going to do it." That worked well for her, she said, until the person wanted to engage in something softer.

Gradually, Beth found significant healing, which she considers an ongoing and lifelong process. She credits several modalities for her growth, particularly individual therapy. The same therapist has helped her manage trauma related to two abusive relationships, as well as her childhood traumas. Whenever something doesn't feel right in her life, she phones the therapist and works on processing, awareness, and getting back on track.

Beth also works with an energy healer who helps her protect her energy and maintain boundaries, given her tendency to help and give to others to extreme degrees. It takes more than verbally saying no, she said, because she's prone to giving too much of her energy away while absorbing that of others. Once a month, she meets with the healer, who provides reiki therapy, cranial work, and chakra realignment using special stones. "I don't know all too much about each stone and the purpose and how that works and the different tools that she uses," Beth added, "but she is also Indigenous and has been doing healing work in the community for a very long time. She's a very trusted resource."

Beth credits learning about intergenerational trauma and connecting to her identity as a Native woman for her ability to thrive and evolve too. One of the biggest elements has been connecting with her ancestors, especially her grandmother, whom she remained physically close to until her last breath in Beth's early twenties. "Even beyond her physical presence here on this earth, I very much connect with her spiritually," she said. "I'm very intuitive and I also get a lot of guidance from her in various ways. I connect a lot with dreaming—not necessarily daydreaming, but like being in a restful state and being able to connect with ancestors that way. And although there's a lot of trauma experienced by my family members, for hundreds of years, there's also a lot of strength there. And so I really belong to that strength."

Since Beth was a child, her grandmother reminded her that she comes from a long line of Navajo women, matriarchs who can handle anything. "So in moments that I've ever felt down or a bit defeated, I have to remember that," she said. "And also, when we think of the genocide of Native people in this country, knowing that I'm one of the very few . . . I come from a family who has survived so much. We almost didn't exist and we do, and I'm part of that lineage that's still here. So there's a lot of strength in that. Sometimes I really pull on that."

Jamila's Reflections

Using paradox as a foundational concept can often be an unexpected source of strength, particularly when we are dealing with the huge, long-standing impact of White supremacy and intergenerational trauma. So many of us live in at least two worlds, the larger world of dominant culture and the world of our cultural upbringing. Most of us have to live and work within these larger systems. In order to have food to eat and a place to live, we are forever engaging with systems that were not designed to support and care for folks marginalized by race, economic status, gender, ability, etc. And yet we learn to live and love within these systems. Allowing ourselves to acknowledge that there is a both-ness to our lives can help us identify and understand our experience.

Paradox has also been useful as a way of drawing strength and support from our cultural and/or religious traditions. In Beth's story, although it was someone from within her culture and family who harmed her and others, it was her cultural connections and other family that offered support and care and protection. Often at the beginning of the clinical journey with clients, many of them feel a (justifiable) rage toward or alienation from their religion or cultural background. There's a narrative of reactive pain: If I separate myself, I'll be OK. Or conversely, they feel that they have to cling even more tightly to that religion or background. I believe either narrative is protective and should be honored and held gently.

Grounding Exercise

Think about a flavor you really enjoy, or actually taste something, such as a mint or a crisp apple if you have one nearby. Notice everything you can about the textures, flavors, and any other sensations that arise. Close your eyes to heighten your sense of taste.

7

"They Don't Understand."

For many, many years, extremely little was broadly known about trauma. And much of what was alluded to involved soldiers having been exposed to or involved in traumatic war events. When PTSD was finally added to the *Diagnostic and Statistical Manual of Mental Disorders* in 1980, it remained controversial. In the 1700s, symptoms of PTSD in war veterans were described as "nostalgia," followed by "soldier's heart" or "irritable heart" to describe symptoms such as a rapid pulse, breathing changes, and anxiety. In the early 1900s, "shell shock" was used to describe PTSD symptoms because they were believed to stem from explosions of artillery shells.

Today, far more is known and accepted about the psychological impact of trauma, whether related to war or not. Trauma is broadly accepted as something legitimate, and traumatic events and experiences are generally known to affect people differently, both in the medical community and everyday conversations. Experts such as Bessel van der Kolk, MD, Dr. Nadine Burke Harris, Dan Siegel, Pat Ogden, PhD, and many others have been profoundly instrumental in bringing this knowledge to popular awareness. While all of that is positive and helps people feel less "broken" or alone, it is still common for survivors to experience some amount of "they don't understand" from family, friends, and even among medical/mental health care providers along the way. In some cases, this derives from not understanding that something that happened indeed was traumatic—if the trauma, say, involved inappropriate touch versus rape, for example, or witnessing someone else's assault rather than experiencing it firsthand. Others aren't likely to understand our trigger flares when we haven't recognized them as such just yet. In terms of understanding and implementing trauma-informed care, there is still considerable work to be done in shifting from a more behavioral/mechanistic paradigm to one that honors multiplicity and acknowledges that experiencing trauma has a great deal to do with what resources and supports we have access to or have been systematically denied access to.

It can also take a while for an individual to recognize trauma reactions as just that. They might not yet realize that when their partner pulls away during sex as a trauma response, for example, it has nothing to do with rejection and everything to do with the brain and body recalling and reacting to past events as though they've become present tense.

When a loved one inadvertently triggers us or doesn't seem to understand why we're reacting to certain stimuli the way we do, it's important that we aim to get to a place of mutual understanding, so that even if they don't know all the details, they can support us in ways that truly help. If that doesn't happen, a perpetual lack of understanding can lead to self-blame, isolation, and resentment, all of which can be devastating for the person experiencing the effects of trauma and for the relationship as a whole.

Sadly, there are people who do not want to believe survivors of trauma, often because they don't want to believe that the atrocity happened. While that doesn't justify a person's unwillingness to understand what happened or justify outright victim-blaming, knowing that may provide some useful perspective. The person may not believe you out of fear that the truth will somehow shatter their worldview. In many other cases, the person who doesn't understand needs proper guidance and education so that they can offer support. In other words, it's not that they don't want to understand. They just literally don't (yet). People in marginalized populations tend to face a lack of understanding the most, when racialized tropes stand in the way. A Black man, for example, is supposed to be "strong" and stoic, according to common societal messaging. So if he reveals that he has been abused or shows vulnerability or feelings of distress around trauma, someone who has absorbed these messages might dismiss those feelings, rather than offer deserved and needed support. Someone in the LGBTQIA+ population might reveal their true identity to a loved one, only to have the information chalked up to "a phase," which is also harmful and commonly stems from societal or cultural beliefs. In those circumstances, too, hope for positive change exists, as long as the person is willing to unpack the messaging they've absorbed and learn and embrace a better path. As a survivor, it's important to know that changing another person's views is not your responsibility. And if someone doesn't believe you, finding someone who does, someone who understands or wants to understand, is a crucial first step toward moving forward.

As sociologist and author Brené Brown, PhD, illustrates in her work, empathy is available to all of us, even if we haven't gone through precisely what another person has. Empathy means, "I understand your experience from your context" or "I'm listening for your context so that I can understand it from your viewpoint." It doesn't mean, "I have lived through that, therefore I understand." That kind of empathetic listening is one of the greatest gifts we can give to another person who is dealing with the effects of trauma, and one of the greatest gifts we can receive when we're struggling. Empathy can be profoundly healing, paving the way for stronger connection and intimacy with others, as well as the sincere feeling and belief that we are worthy of pleasure.

TAYLOR: LIFESAVING PSYCHIATRY AND DEVELOPING HER TRUE SELF

Taylor Lianne Chandler describes herself as having textbook borderline personality disorder: strong fears of abandonment, harmful impulsive behaviors, chronic feelings of worthlessness, and an unstable sense of self that fueled the perceived need to morph into the person others wanted her to be in any given situation. For decades, however, the disorder went untreated. She was twenty-eight years old and going through a divorce from an abusive partner in 2000 when she finally had a name for her intense struggles she experienced over the years. And like many people with borderline personality disorder (BPD), her symptoms are rooted in trauma. Enduring ten years of molestation and incest during her childhood led her to drink excessively, use drugs, and do virtually anything she could to "get outside of [her] head and feel something."

For seven years, she engaged in sex work, where she said she learned not to trust men, given that most of her clients were married and having sex with another woman in secret. While not all sex workers have that same experience or perspective, witnessing serial dishonesty in any context can shape our worldviews and contribute to trauma. If a child's mother, aunt, and grandmother cheated on their respective partners, for example, it might be difficult for the child to trust women. During that time period, Taylor was raped at gunpoint and beaten nearly to death when a man realized she was transgender. He spouted out Bible verses as he attacked her. He was arrested, charged, and sentenced to three to seven years for use of a firearm but nothing for the rape. Because of a mistrial, she had to endure the court proceedings twice.

Seven years had passed when she sat in a psychiatrist's office and received her diagnosis for BPD. While she kept it to herself because of pervasive stigma, she sought counseling and took prescribed medications that seemed to really help. After two years of consistent treatment, though, she was doing so well that she believed she could stop going to therapy and taking her medication. So with her therapist's go-ahead, she did. From there, things gradually became untethered again. Then, some six years ago, they took a sharp turn for the worse. "All of my worlds came crashing together, because part of borderline is adapting and becoming whatever's needed for the situation," she said. "And in 2014, I was stripped of that ability. My whole life was made public, and so there was no becoming anybody. There was no disguising." She was dating and in love with a world-famous athlete when this "crashing" happened. The media learned of the relationship and outed her as intersex, something she hadn't yet felt comfortable sharing with many people, much less the world. Then the man denied their relationship, a form of trans erasure that still pains her to this day.

Taylor's traumas and the unmanaged BPD they fueled impacted her relationships with sex, pleasure, and others significantly for much of her life. "I often describe borderline like the *Runaway Bride*," she explained. "If you watched how she dated the men, whoever she dated, that's how she liked her eggs. That's what she got interested in.

That's how she'd wear her hair. That's borderline." Because of that, she said, she never really developed her own personality. And rather than enjoy sex, she learned to use it as a weapon or tool.

When intimate details from her life were put under a microscope on a grand scale and misinformation spread like a hurtful game of telephone in a media frenzy, she began slipping into one of her deepest lows. She attempted many types of treatments for her BPD and nothing seemed to help. Her mental state pulled her into anorexia, at one point landing her in a hospital on feeding tubes. One day, she knew she could not take the struggles anymore. She told a doctor that she didn't want to die, but she had no desire to live. That doctor referred her to a psychiatrist who prescribed a combination of medications that turned out to be near-miraculous. "Within like three days, my whole world changed," she said. "And it was almost like I could look back on my old life and I was viewing it as a bystander."

When a short-lived romantic relationship didn't work out a few months later, she was stunned by how she felt. While it was challenging, there were no world-shattering abandonment feelings making it impossible for her to function. No "life or death" thoughts or self-hatred. She could let the relationship go and move on with her life. That relationship also helped her see what a healthy relationship feels like in comparison to the abusive partnerships she felt trapped in during her most vulnerable states.

There have been times when her medications needed adjustments or when she has feared that they'll simply stop working. The medications that help her so deeply also cause some limitations in her emotional range, keeping her from being able to cry, for example. But overall, Taylor has never felt so balanced or healthy. She now works in HIV prevention and speaks publicly about transgender rights. She's married to a wonderful man, who brought two children into her life.

"I never dreamed I'd be in a place where I'm actually in a marriage with someone who I love and they love me back," she said of her earlier days. "I never dreamed of the day where I would want sex or enjoy it. I always saw it as a chore, or a means to an end or, like I said, a weapon . . . but now my marriage is real and I deal with real emotions. I have multiple orgasms with my husband and I love sex."

EL: EMBRACING DESIRES AND SEXUALITY INTEGRATION

EL never thought much about whether or not his level of desire for sex was "normal" until he entered into a romantic relationship, and then another, that turned out to be harmful. Both partners shamed him for what he now perceives as a higher than average sex drive, using it as "a vehicle for mental and emotional abuse." Both of his first two partners would police his sexuality and libido, he said, putting him down whenever he expressed attraction to other people, while "simultaneously engaging in unethical non-monogamy practices," stepping outside the boundaries they had agreed on. "I was made to feel as though my sex drive would mean that I would never find a partner who was satisfied with me, or who would satisfy me," he said, "and this was used as a means of manipulation and control." As a result, he's grappled with notions that his sexuality is his prominent, and sometimes only, means of acceptance and validation.

For EL, the "honeymoon phase" of a relationship never dies down in terms of sex, in terms of his desires. For him, sexual connection with others fuels emotional connection—like the opposite end of a spectrum that goes from demisexuality to his orientation. Now that he's embraced polyamory, he can better thrive. At the same time, he doesn't feel he can be open about that part of his identity. "I already struggled with so many aspects of feeling marginalized because I'm a person of color, I'm clergy in a liberal religious tradition. So I can't be open about my polyamory," he said. "There's a little bit of . . . not necessarily shame, but it's more like, do I want to confirm that I'm part of yet another marginalized group? I don't know."

EL has never knowingly pressured a partner into more sex or any sexual activity than they're comfortable with, prizing consent and respect above all and being a highly empathetic person. Meanwhile, he cannot feel satisfied or fulfilled with one partner, particularly if that partner desires less sex than he does, which has consistently been the case. Still, the shame caused by his first two intimate relationships lingers on. And when he doesn't have access to sex, such as during the COVID-19 pandemic, he has felt broken, crying on his primary partner's shoulder and wondering, "Why can't I just be normal?"

Masturbation sometimes takes a bit of the edge off when he's under high levels of stress, which bolsters his desires, but it doesn't suffice. "I am unable to have an orgasm from penetrative sex, period . . . so sexual connection for me has always been about the act not the end," he said. He seldom experiences orgasm at all during sex, something that's seldom discussed in the context of cisgender men. "It's had this weird effect that I never would have thought with some partners who actually get really annoyed or angry at me because I can't orgasm," he said. "And it's like, 'I told you in the beginning. This is just how I am. This is not about you.'" Other partners really appreciate this about EL, because sex can last as long as they'd like.

Having an especially high libido can seem problematic in all genders, he noted, because of cultural messaging. "Society sees women with high sex drives as being 'slutty,' you know, like they can't be faithful," he said. "Men buy into this idea that men are always supposed to be horny. And so when they're not, there's a significant amount of shame about, 'Do I admit that?'" He's also heard from many men who have a lower sex drive than their female partner and struggle with not wanting to admit it and feeling like less of a man. "On the flip side, I feel broken because I'm like, 'What is with my wiring that this is this is something that I always need?'"

It wasn't until EL began therapy that he realized his first two romantic relationships were abusive. That understanding, as well as owning the abuse as part of his experience, really helped. "Because admitting being the victim of abuse is heavily looked down upon in cis males in heteronormative relationships, there was a great deal of struggle to break through this bias," he said. "Once I did, though, it opened a lot of doors for healing and introspection."

Before the pandemic, his level of confidence and self-acceptance in realizing he isn't sexually flawed had shifted to a healthy, stable place, he recalled. Once the lockdowns and social distancing were in place, limiting his access to other partners while his nesting partner endures health problems that make sex unfeasible, he's felt unable to cope. "It's a huge fucking struggle," he shared. "I mean, I have a sex therapist that I specifically sought out . . . for general therapy, but this is also a component of who I am. I have friends that I talk to that are very compassionate and empathetic about it. But at the end of the day, it's been up to me to just deal with it."

EL said he wanted to share his story because he knows from experience that shame around sexual desires can lead folks down a dangerous path. Two years ago, he was nearly kicked out of school when high amounts of stress and internalized shame around his resultant increased need for sex took away from his ability to thrive. "I worked in an addiction treatment center for a year as a spiritual counselor, so I'm familiar with the theories behind addiction," he said. "And I as I look back, I was using sex the way an addict would use a substance in order to ignore, in this case, all of my schoolwork. I wasn't engaging in risky behavior, so much as any opportunity for sex that that seemed even halfway plausible I would jump at to the point of ignoring everything else in my life."

If we don't embrace healthy aspects of our sexuality as natural parts of who we are, we can easily perceive them as "deviant or wrong," he said. "Then you drift into doing some really unhealthy things." Bottling up his desires after his first two partners essentially said, *I put up with your problematic sexuality and the rest of the world won't* prompted him to try to stifle his yearnings "until they all just explode." When we instead integrate our sexuality into our lives and accept ourselves for who we are sexually, the possibilities of growth, pleasure, and deeper connections with ourselves and others are virtually endless.

Jamila's Reflections

EL's story underscores the importance of understanding our sexuality and having compassion for the incredible diversity of how our bodies work, how our desire works, and the different levels of desire we experience. When we don't have a sense of legitimacy of our sexual response or our sexual desire, as EL said, we can drift into trying to clamp it down or control it or we believe the damaging stories that others tell us about our sexuality.

One of the most exciting ideas about sexuality as a concept is the idea of biodiversity. Life itself thrives when we have variety in our lives. Nature abhors a vacuum and only one kind of anything existing is the sign of stagnation, not health. And so, if we take that lesson and understand the ways that we work and the ways life may have influenced our sexuality, we can understand that our desires are legitimate, as long as there is communication, consent, and trust. What's most important is your contribution to the biodiversity of sexual identity, gender, and sexual response.

EL also brings up these ideas of hypersexuality or hyposexuality, which is to say that we have these medicalized ideas that there is somehow a "normal" sexuality and a "normal" sex drive. There isn't. Some people want a lot; some people want a little. Compared to another person in a relationship, there will always be a difference because there are two or more different people. And that's OK. What's important is figuring out how to respectfully navigate that and to not pathologize or problematize the differences, but to have empathy for them, and to figure out how to navigate the different needs and desires of the people involved in the relationship.

As the social and biological underpinnings of sexuality continue to be explored and more continues to be learned, we're figuring out that there's this expansive sense of sexuality, as opposed to "normal' or "abnormal." Neither of these terms provide a helpful or accurate frame, and both can fuel emotional pain and trauma while standing in the way of pleasure, connection, and authenticity. One example of a "norm" that isn't accurate is highlighted by the fact that some cis men do not ejaculate with penetration or through oral sex, and that's simply how their bodies work. There is nothing wrong with them or their partners. It can be very exciting to separate ideas of orgasm, ejaculation, pleasure, and connection. These are all different elements of sexual experiences, and we don't need to have every single one of them in order for a sexual experience to be satisfying. In fact, there are lots of books and videos for people who are curious about learning how cis men can have multiple orgasms and how to separate ejaculation from orgasm. There's a whole world of information out there. I encourage you to have fun, explore, and simply see what's out there without feeling the need to match up to factors considered "normal." We want you to practice learning to trust yourself and your body, to go have fun or explore with your body and/or the bodies of your lover(s).

One of the ways that EL discovered a new way of thinking about his sexuality and his body was through his practice of polyamory. And while polyamory, relationship anarchy, and other types of consensual non-monogamy aren't ideal for everybody or for every relationship, they are valid and ideal for those who desire them. One of the great gifts that many people discover with consensual non-monogamy is that they have an expanded sense of relationships with others—that different aspects of ourselves that can be amplified or explored with other people. Monogamy has wonderful attributes as well, and one can explore one's emotional and sexual desires within monogamy and/or through cultivating friendships that allow for intimacy, connection, exploration, and discovery. Polyamory as a relationship style is an equally legitimate way of connecting with other people, and not because something is wrong with their primary relationship but because some of us are interested in the variety of different kinds of relationships, that may or may not be sexual or romantic, but that can absolutely be fulfilling and supportive.

Whether you are interested in consensual non-monogamy or not, I invite you to remember that isolation is one of the most dangerous states to be in. Humans were never meant to exist alone in isolation or in fear from others. We thrive when we are in community and in connection with others who help us create spaces in which we can see our similarities *and* our differences. So whatever kind of relationship style you're interested in, continue to practice and seek community and connection with other people. That is one of the keys to a healthy and vibrant life.

Depending on factors such as the jobs that we have, our families of origin, and the places we live, we may not be or feel free to be out about the different parts of how we have sex or how we do our relationships. I want to express that that's OK. Sometimes circumstances change and we get more tools, more support, or our environment shifts in some way so that we can be further who we are. But sometimes that's just not possible, given societal structures and certain kinds of stigma that will affect our health, finances, and even our safety. We absolutely encourage you to find the supports that you can, whether that's a therapist or one or two friends whom you can be completely transparent with and who support you in your journey. Finding those little cracks in between what may seem immovable is how we survive and then learn how to thrive in extraordinarily challenging circumstances.

FINDING THOSE LITTLE CRACKS IN BETWEEN WHAT MAY SEEM IMMOVABLE IS HOW WE SURVIVE AND THEN LEARN HOW TO THRIVE IN EXTRAORDINARILY CHALLENGING CIRCUMSTANCES.

Grounding Exercise

Visualize a task. Choose a routine task you enjoy or don't mind doing. Maybe that's decorating for a particular holiday, washing dishes, or folding freshly washed clothes. Imagine each step and all of the senses the task engages—the look of holiday lights, the scent of dish soap, the warmth of clean clothing. Close your eyes and state the steps aloud, if that helps, or jot them down on a notepad or computer document.

8

"How Can I Get My Life Back?"

When something painful happens, it's natural to reflect on and long for a time machine of sorts—anything to allow us to leap, beam, or fly our way back to life *before it all changed*. Before triggers became routine. Before the nightmares, the fits of sobs, the exhaustion. Longing to go back to life before a particular trauma unfolded makes sense. Why *wouldn't* we wish for less struggle? Those longings, as common and reasonable as they may be, aren't terribly helpful from a healing or growth perspective. The good news is that while we can't go back, or snap our fingers to change the societal systems that fuel trauma and desperately need change, we can move forward and, over time, create something beautifully rich in our lives.

Post-traumatic growth (PTG) is a theory developed in the mid-1990s by psychologists Lawrence Calhoun, PhD, and Richard Tedeschi, PhD. But folks have likely been experiencing it for centuries. In an interview with the American Psychological Association, Kanako Taku, PhD, an associate professor of psychology at Oakland University, noted that PTG is often considered synonymous with resilience, but it's more than that. Taku experienced PTG herself after enduring Japan's Kobe earthquake in 1995. While "resiliency is the personal attribute or ability to bounce back," said Taku, PTG involves difficulties that challenge your core beliefs after experiencing trauma, but then ultimately cultivates a sense of profound personal growth.

It isn't a quick or automatic shift. Rather, it requires "a lot of time, energy, and struggle." In other words, the challenges we live with because of trauma don't prevent growth or resiliency. They can, however, help make way for them over time when you practice integrating helpful tools into your life. And prioritizing self-love and pleasure in our lives can strengthen this process by first strengthening our relationship with ourselves. The rewards of all of this work aren't a cure-all, but they still might surpass your wildest imaginings.

KIMLEIGH: YOU ARE YOUR OWN SUPERHERO

Kimleigh Smith described her childhood self as a "girl with just lots of positive energy." She was creative, outgoing, and a cheerleader. Most everything but math was her jam. Growing up Black on an ethnically diverse military base in Japan with parents who encouraged the acceptance of others, she said, made way for shock upon arriving in the United States at age ten, where people took issue with her color. Because she had White friends in Kansas, people often said she wasn't "*that* kind of Black," the sort that only hung out with "their kind," which she described as "such a disservice to Black women."

Looking back, Kimleigh considers herself a late bloomer, in terms of dating and intimacy, while her voluptuous breasts grew early. When boys and men took notice, she didn't quite understand the attention. "They'd always say, 'Oh my God, you got some nice packs,' and I thought they were talking about my biceps. So I was like, 'Oh, thank you!'" she recalled. "I was such a nerd ball around men. I really didn't have sex in high school . . . I was the girl that nobody chose, and not because they didn't like me, but just because I was such a powerful energy."

"If you read my yearbook, you'd be like, 'Oh my God, that girl was loved,'" she said. "But if I'm to be super honest, I was always really, really afraid of boys." The night before Kimleigh left for college, at age seventeen, she went on her first date with a friend she'd had a crush on for some time. When he tried to kiss her, she nearly froze in fear, given her inexperience and the S. E. X. she knew kisses could lead to. Those same factors led her to feel awkward and "nerdy" on the university campus. Yet people assumed she was sexually experienced, assumptions likely fueled by the fetishization of large breasts and Blackness and perhaps notions that vivaciousness in women and femmes equals sexual fervency. She wouldn't realize until much later that inappropriate touch by an extended relative—not molestation, but seemingly an attempt—which was normalized, played a role in her fears around men, sex, and intimacy.

Her first experience with overt "sexual anything" was deeply traumatic. During college, she was gang-raped, an assault she dissociated from out of self-preservation. It was "almost like a blackout," she said; her memory of that day started immediately after the attack, when she walked to the shower to cleanse away blood. When a friend told her that the rapists were bragging about a supposed threesome they'd had with her, she had no clear memory of anything sex-related having happened.

Throughout the years that followed, Kimleigh said she knew something was off. So emotionally paralyzed, she couldn't experience healthy, pleasurable sex. Meanwhile, she entered beauty pageants and continued cheerleading, then attained a degree in psychology. Throughout all four years of college and four of her seven years of living in Chicago, she recalls being in "full repression," engaging in what she described as "self-destructive sex." She had to dissociate and felt "nothing" in her body. Soon, clearer memories started to resurface, haunting her days and dreams.

After negative experiences with wrong-fit therapists, a friend suggested she try hypnotherapy, a methodology that can instill a therapeutic sense of mindfulness and may help positively restructure traumatic memories when you work with a credible professional. While Kimleigh still doesn't recall every detail of the rape, this treatment helped her fully accept what had happened.

"This is mine," she said of the impact of that acceptance. "It's my journey, and I receive it. I respect it. I see it. And I send love and light and healing to the boys who did this to me, because they were hurting themselves to be able to put themselves in a situation to do that to me. That's their stuff to carry."

Today, Kimleigh no longer feels ashamed when she feels triggered, which happens less often, but feels challenging nonetheless. Being activated during a very meaningful sexual experience in recent years helped bring more healing than pain. "This was the first time I realized that [dissociating] was self-preservation through all of my lifetime, and I could cry when I think about it because I spent so many years thinking I was broken sexually, and I was always very able to have sex if it didn't feel emotionally vulnerable . . . the person didn't mean enough to fear losing. And this guy meant enough to me. If I lost him, it would mean everything." Through nurturing herself, she was able to open her heart to another, allowing more love to flow in.

If you're a fellow survivor and just starting your healing journey or wishing for more pleasurable sex, Kimleigh suggests having a loving conversation with yourself. "Our mind is such a powerful tool that can shut us down at the moment's notice," she added. "You know, if you have ever had a great orgasm, it comes when you let it all go. And so it really becomes finding a way to heal yourself, to forgive yourself, so that you can feel free again."

Kimleigh's Mirror Exercise

Stand before a mirror and look yourself in the eyes. From there, start a loving conversation with yourself, as though you're speaking to a beloved friend. Stay there for as little or as long as you feel comfortable, using words of self-love, self-compassion, and self-forgiveness, such as:

"Even if you don't believe it yet, you are worthy of love."

"I want to take care of you."

"I'm not giving up on you."

"I love you."

"I forgive you."

"When I first started this, I couldn't look at myself for more than one second without bawling," Kimleigh said. "Now I can have a whole hour conversation with myself and I love myself." She has found that this process can really foster self-compassion and freedom when you feel a sense of self-shame after enduring something traumatic. In particular, she recommends this mirror exercise for anyone who struggles with discomfort around solo or partnered sex.

Now an author, international speaker, actress, and sex-positive sexual assault advocate, Kimleigh remains dedicated to helping people discover and embrace the superhero within themselves: to own their story, reclaim their power, and cultivate emotional freedom. While she wouldn't wish the attack and trauma she has experienced on anyone, she said, embracing it as part of her journey has felt important. "The moment I got off that floor, I was a survivor and the woman I am today is a thriver," she said. "We survived the moment. We didn't die in that moment. And we stood up and we walked out. We walked away or we crawled away. Or we found ourselves on the floor, like I did, bleeding. The moment I stood up, I knew I'd already survived and I spent my whole life being something more than a survivor, being a thriver, who lives an awesome life." And she hopes that by sharing her story, you'll feel permitted to "live awesomely" too.

Jamila's Reflections

As we discussed earlier in this chapter, resilience is different from post-traumatic growth, and it is not a requirement for wanting to have a different kind of life or wanting to move further into your own healing in the next stage of your life. We are also not suggesting that your trauma made you able to be "phenomenal" or "amazing." It's also important to make room for the fact that we are never going to have the lives that we had before our traumas. That is a hard truth, but it is true nonetheless. That does not mean, however, that we can't have an amazing, rich life, and an intentional life full of joy and community. These things can absolutely happen.

If we continue to create a society in which people have access to different kinds of support and care, we can emerge with more nuance, more awareness, more compassion, and increased skill sets around how to navigate relationships after a trauma. We can use what we've learned in managing our trauma and moving with it to find and create something rich and worth having. At the same time, I don't ever want to push the idea that experiencing trauma itself makes somebody better. It doesn't. Trauma is painful and no matter what you have lived through or are living through, you don't deserve it. You deserve to have a life in which you feel safe and cared for and where you can trust the systems and people around you. To some extent, we can create that, but we are living in a time and place in which we cannot always rely on the systems of power around us.

Contained within Kimleigh's story is a beautiful awareness that every moment that you continue to survive to find a way to feed yourself, to get a little bit of rest, to connect with others, to learn about yourself, to move forward in your life, is magnificent and beautiful and important. Your ways of surviving can keep you alive long enough to lead to a place where you can now train yourself to thrive. When I sit across from my clients, I am in awe of their creativity, their accrued abilities, and their willingness to continue on in the face of incredibly limited support and harshness and continual onslaughts to their sense of self. They show up when they can and in the ways that they can, and they remind me all the time of how incredible the human spirit is. So you might have very hard days, where life doesn't feel like it matters, when it doesn't seem like anyone cares. Please know that anything that you do to keep resting and resisting until you can move forward again is a magnificent affirmation of the value of your life and every one of those steps matters.

ANYTHING THAT YOU DO TO KEEP RESTING UNTIL YOU CAN MOVE FORWARD AGAIN IS A MAGNIFICENT AFFIRMATION OF THE VALUE OF YOUR LIFE AND EVERY ONE OF THOSE STEPS MATTERS.

A NOTE ABOUT MIRROR WORK

When we learn to see ourselves, not through the distorted visions of the pain that people have put us in, but learn to see our bodies and our faces and our humanity undistorted, unharmed, and unwarped by ideas of thinness or fatness or what an "acceptable" body is or what an "acceptable" hair texture is, when we can move through the process of looking in a mirror and see exactly what is there, which is your glorious humanity and your glorious contribution to the diversity of humanity, that is powerful work. When you can look in a mirror and smile at yourself and see nothing but the magnificence that is you.

If you are curious about mirror work, move into that space and try it. Perhaps you have a friend who does something similar and with whom you can compare notes afterward. This is simply one method among many to see what will be supportive to you. As always, pay attention to what pulls you, and if it worries you or scares you a little bit, decide if you want to continue.

Mirror work is powerful and intense, and it is a process. I really liked that Kimleigh discovered this way of speaking to and with herself. Powerful revelations and confidence can come from this very slow, intense, and sometimes even frightening experience of really looking at ourselves and allowing ourselves to see what's there. If you are going to engage in mirror work, I encourage you to do it in small amounts and to have some sort of structure around how you're going to move into it at the beginning and what you're going to do for yourself after. And if you find yourself getting frightened or you have bad thoughts, it's absolutely OK to stop and to never pick it up again, or to pick it up again at a later time. Remember that we're learning to practice pleasure and to practice curiosity about what is.

ARDEN: AWARENESS, MAGIC, AND SEXUAL NARRATIVES

Arden Leigh grew up in the suburbs of Philadelphia, where she attended Catholic school. She considers security in her mother's love one of her biggest blessings. Part of their bond stemmed from having a common enemy: Arden's abusive father.

"If you crossed Donald Trump with the Incredible Hulk, you would get my dad," she said, "all the pathological lying and narcissism and acting like a victim, like, 'Oh, nothing's ever my fault.'" While she said many people assume that her trauma derives solely from her father's abuse, Arden considers her core wounds to be rooted in the failure of other adults in her life to believe her amid the abuse. Although her mother was an exception, believing and intimately understanding Arden's trials, she had little power against legal proceedings that relied on "he said/she said" (a notion that tends to be based largely on a lack of thorough investigation) and ultimately decided that her pleas didn't warrant any changes. Moving forward, she still had to see her dad every other weekend and during one- to two-week vacation periods. Guidance counselors, nuns at her school, and psychological evaluators believed his words over Arden's too.

And so, Arden took to trying to prove herself valuable and believable in other ways, becoming a "perfect student" in her youth and later attempting to convince boys, and later men, that she was worth dating. She was nine when her parents divorced, something she was thrilled about until a harsh new reality set in: she would have to spend time with her father alone, away from her mom. Arden eventually tried to obtain legal emancipation from her father, but that didn't pan out. These collective wounds were exacerbated by additional traumas in her adulthood, including being persecuted for sex work after a major newspaper outed her as a pro domme, being raped by a boss, and dating an emotionally abusive celebrity. By the time that relationship started, she had transitioned from BDSM work into teaching seduction work in the pickup artist field, where her strong urge to please others continued.

"I knew the pickup stuff, but I was more into, you know, 'Create your seductive persona' and 'live larger than life,'" she said. "I kind of put all of that energy of BDSM into this idea of finding people who don't necessarily identify as dominant, but who maybe want to play with it and play with BDSM in a way that I can provide since I'm experienced in it, and subvert all my submissiveness into seduction, which is essentially people-pleasing."

Rather than engage in these modalities for pleasure, eroticism, and empowerment, as many kinksters do, Arden said she used kink, submission, and seduction to try to earn her place in the abusive relationship. That relationship was kept a secret, which she considered justified at the time, given that the man was so well-known, working for a "large, family-friendly media corporation," and was going through a divorce. That divorce was kept private until long after his breakup with Arden. Later, he left Arden for a "super vanilla, super monogamous" woman. Being known as someone who embraces less traditional notions of sex and relationships still isn't largely accepted in Hollywood.

"He had all these fantasies that he wanted to explore," she recalled. "So I provided that. . . . We got to do all these really fun, kinky, sexy things together. We almost created a whole narrative world of our relationship. And that was really beautiful, but it was the thing that I was doing for *him*. And the space that I was holding for him. As soon as he could be in what he considered a legit relationship again, he just dropped me."

Looking back, Arden feels she enabled codependent behavior in the relationship with "the narrative of BDSM," figuring its harmful experiences were normal in the kink world, because her relationships were "committed fantasies where [she] didn't really have any needs." "I fetishized my own suffering as part of the kink," she added. "I told myself that endurance made me strong. That narrative was dangerous for me because it enabled my own inability to set boundaries and justified it as submission."

It took Arden a long time to recognize the man's behaviors throughout the relationship as abuse, she said, largely because, compared to her father, he seemed normal. She now believes that it's important for all trauma survivors to examine their sexual narratives, a process she has found profoundly helpful in her own journey. One major epiphany around this took place when she joined the #YesAllWomen campaign, sharing her experiences with trauma at the hands of men online. When she did, men's responses were enraging.

"Previously they said, 'Oh, Arden is so hot. She's like the girl pickup artist and she writes articles about how to give a better blow job,'" she added. "The minute I started talking about Yes, All Women, all these dudes . . . were like, 'I'm tuning you out. I used to think you were cool, but now you just turned into another feminazi like all the others.' And I'm just like, '*Are you fucking kidding me?* I have spent the last years of my life appealing to your needs and teaching other women how to appeal your needs . . . and the minute that I start to speak up about my experience as a woman, you can't hold space for that?'"

That experience served as a wake-up call for Arden, after she had invested so much energy in creating her identity as "the cool girl," she said. This happened during 2016, not long before Trump was voted into office. And similar to the experience of many women and LGBTQIA+ folks, this felt like a personal affront to Arden. "It was like this amazing parallel in my life, of me letting the dominant, straight, White dudes in my life run the relationships, run us into the ground, and put us in these toxic situations. . . . And it's the same thing that's happening in our country. [They] are not looking out for us." At that point, she left pickup and seduction work.

When Arden sought therapy, none of the professionals she saw perceived or addressed her trauma, she said, wanting to treat her for anxiety and depression instead. It wasn't until she moved to the West Coast and started engaging in spiritual and witchcraft circles for social reasons that she started to realize that trauma underlaid her challenges. "I was like, 'I'll do some fun things, meet some fun girls, chant around the bonfire, or whatever,'" she recalled. "And they ended up changing my life."

"There's this thing that happens when you start doing magic that's in alignment with your higher self and . . . your highest good," she said. "Things just start flowing differently." In addition to finding and staying committed to her own healing, Arden gleaned certifications in alternative healing practices, such as hypnotherapy and reiki, and immersed herself in the study of trauma and attachment styles, and launched a program to help others who feel called to similar modalities and haven't found the support they need elsewhere. Arden also found an example of a man in her life who isn't harmful and who prizes her well-being—Grant Morrison, a magician who taught her magic in exchange for consulting on his *Wonder Woman* book. "I was like, holy shit, OK, I found one," she said. "I found one great guy showing up for me as a friend and being emotionally supportive of me with no agenda. . . . When I found one, I could start seeing more around me, and now I have an abundance of healthy male friendships that have raised the standards of the kind of treatment I know I can expect from a partner. So yeah, it's kind of cool to be transforming your whole life on a very practical, actionable level."

Jamila's Reflections

When we experience a narcissistic parent or parental figure as a child, it can have a profound impact on our expectations about relationships and how we "should" operate within close relationships, whether personal or professional. The kinds of experiences Arden had in finding a cis man who was not only interested in her work but also actively interested in supporting her work and her growth without expectation of emotional labor or sexual labor can be enormously healing, because it disrupts what we've come to expect out of relationships.

Another aspect of Arden's story worth noting is that she experienced feeling let down by the mental health field. Arden was seeking something that therapy could not provide, and the providers that she interacted with did not give her the kind of support that she was looking for. It's so important, as we said before, to know that your healing path and journey toward a pleasurable life are going to be completely unique. We strongly encourage you to weave together the practices, the people, the rituals, and the places that will support you and your own uniqueness. In moving your life in the direction that you want, with the supports that suit you, you are contributing to the diversity of what healing can look like in the world. It's more than OK if somebody chooses not to use traditional mental health services and instead finds other helpful alternatives. As always, we want for you to find the best care that you can, as well as find people who support you to develop your inner sense of confidence, your inner sense of rightness, and your ability to navigate and contribute to the world in your vision—not as a disciple of somebody else, not having to buy your way into different levels of access, but as someone who can simply be encouraged and facilitated to come home to yourself. Life is full of teachers. Find the teachers who really do want the best for you.

LIFE IS FULL OF TEACHERS. FIND THE TEACHERS WHO REALLY DO WANT THE BEST FOR YOU.

One of the most challenging, and yet crucial, lessons of trauma is learning to leave ourselves open to being surprised and to finding exceptions to what we've come to believe about the world. That means that sometimes we may be hurt, but that's not the same as being harmed, and we can still leave ourselves open and permeable enough to allow for new supports to show up and for new people to show up in ways that we could not have imagined when we're in the depths of our trauma response or are seeing the systems of oppression that perpetuate harm. This is not to say to ignore your body signals. Sometimes we need weeks, months, or years of creating and maintaining a protective barrier for certain kinds of people or situations that remind us of our perpetrators, because that's what we need to feel safe enough, to learn to be in our bodies, and to learn to trust ourselves in the world again. That's not wrong. If that never changes for you, that's OK too. There will be other ways of finding healing and other kinds of experiences that you can be open to that will contribute to your sense of agency, wonder, delight, and pleasure. This is not a race, and there is no absolute definition of wellness. There is only you following your curiosity and your pleasure and learning how to create and maintain healthy relationships with and for others. If at some point the walls shift and there's room in your life for a person or situation that reminds you of what has harmed you, that's a decision you can make then. However, that is never a requirement for moving toward and creating a world that centers pleasure and health. Over time, our hope and our invitation is that you'll see that your life has possibility, always, and so healing and new experiences can surprise and delight us and open one more door on our journey toward true renewal and wellness. What that looks like will be up to you.

JAZZ: NO LONGER CONFORMING AND ANCESTRAL AND ANIMIST PRACTICES

Jazz Goldman is a sex educator and performance artist who aims to "deprogram sexual shame, racial violence, imperialist/capitalist mindsets, and gender binary/cis-heteronormativity through community building . . . sex education, performance art, and divine love." Jazz calls this their "soul's work." And their passion and inclination to pursue it all comes from a deeply personal place.

Jazz has managed trauma from multiple experiences, including neglect of their well-being during childhood. "I was never hungry. I never went hungry. I always had clothes. I never worried about if I would have a house to be in and I didn't have those kinds of experiences of neglect or troubles," they said. "But I would experience pain and injuries and my parents would just kind of be checked out or half-notice it." When Jazz needed to start physical therapy for a knee injury during high school, for example, their parents never asked about it or made sure they were doing the required exercises. Then shortly after graduating high school, when they were eighteen, one of Jazz's first sexual partners started choking them during sex without consent. "I was always uncomfortable when it was happening—like, 'Oh, this is hard for me to breathe' uncomfortable," Jazz said. "And I had no kink experience then. Now I know that no one should ever do that without a conversation. There should be safe words and signals and the whole thing."

While living in New York, Jazz entered into a relationship with J. The pair consumed "wild amounts of cannabis" together, all of which was very much under his influence. "I was an adult, about twenty-six, when I was seeing him," Jazz said. "I was not new to cannabis and I already enjoyed it prior to knowing him, but he had a real problem. He could not function in life at all without it." In order to be with him, Jazz felt they had to meet his level of usage. "I didn't understand that that's what was happening," they noted. "That was very much a retrospective, like, 'Oh, I went from this kind of a cannabis consumer to this kind.' I bring that up because it's an important layer. I didn't know that I had any physical traumatic experience with him until way later."

In early adulthood, Jazz moved from New York to Seattle. During their first five months in the new city, they planned a trip to rejoin E, someone they had met in Costa Rica the previous spring. They'd only interacted twice during that trip. And yet Jazz and E felt they were in love. During the trip, the sex they engaged in caused Jazz intense vaginal pain, which they felt they needed to ignore. "I ended up getting sick the next day," Jazz added. "I went from painful sex to a swollen abdomen. I thought it was a water bug that I picked up. . . . But when I finally came back to the states three weeks later and went to the gynecologist, they were like, 'You probably had a cyst burst.'"

A few weeks after the Costa Rica trip, Jazz started dating someone new, a far gentler person. At one point early on, during sex, the non-binary masc-presenting person was touching Jazz with his fingers and seemed to open a flap in their vagina. At the same time, Jazz experienced a "closing situation internally." Looking back, Jazz believes this all stemmed from vaginismus, or involuntary contractions that sometimes happen in response to trauma. The body remembers past pain and clenches up in an attempt to prevent more pain. "I had these really bad experiences in Costa Rica and my body had a hard time with it," Jazz reflected. "But I just didn't acknowledge it because of my own ideas of what my sexuality needed to be—which was that I needed to be able to perform. So it didn't matter if I was experiencing burning sensations or uncomfortable friction. I liked sex, I liked fucking hard. And so I thought that's just what you have to deal with."

In addition to these traumas, Jazz has experience being queer and of mixed race in a cis-dominant, oppressive social scene. "I am Black and Jewish, but I was raised in almost exclusively White environments, and all my friends and lovers until a certain point were all White," they recalled, adding that their non-monogamy community in New York was all White, when they entered it around 2006, as well as largely heteronormative and not very kink-friendly. "Picture me at nineteen with all the eagerness and none of the experience, wanting all of the experience, and really just constantly minimizing whatever didn't seem like it fit well."

These messages prompted Jazz to hide aspects of their sexuality and gender expression. Jazz knew they loved androgyny and spent most of their time in jeans and T-shirts, uninterested in doing away with any body hair, yet they felt the need to shave, wax, apply makeup, and dress up in the typically feminine ways women are expected to for play parties. "I was so desperate for connection," they said. "But as I got older, the friendships were more and more shallow because I was deviating so much from the norm."

When they finally came out as nonbinary-trans-femme to their friends, Jazz was surprised that anyone had missed their true identity. How was this new way of identifying any different from the way they had expressed themself day-to-day before, Jazz would ask, to which those friends would reluctantly agree that it wasn't. Then Jazz would add, "The difference is that I'm refuting the false narratives you're putting on me now instead of buying into them."

Not long after, Jazz volunteered for a trauma support team at a festival for two consecutive years. "That was also really illuminating, just to learn basic techniques for meeting someone who's in a trauma state," they said. "I'm grateful for that experience, but I came out of it almost in worse shape because I had so much undealt-with stuff at the time." That realization set Jazz on the path to truly seeing and unpacking their past traumas. Since then, self-study on trauma, therapy, EMDR, and ancestral and animist spiritual practices have helped Jazz process and manage the effects of those harmful experiences and invite far more pleasure into their life.

Studying ancestral and animist practices have proven especially helpful for Jazz. "I recognize there's a way of seeing the world in which unhealed ancestors in your bloodline will reenact the things that they haven't resolved through you," they said. "It can be almost thought of sometimes as spirit possession, but not like an exorcist possession, where you're literally being moved around. It's more subtle. You're just making choices and having conflicts in your life that in a way are not even yours." In other words, you recognize that some of your difficulties stem not from your own experiences, but those of particular ancestors. You can ask those ancestors to allow you freedom. Similarly, you can trust and rely on the strength and vibrancy of ancestors, feeling their presence, speaking to them, and absorbing their wisdom. Jazz learned how to pray to their own ancestors with the aim of connecting with those who are considered "well and bright"—not bright as in smart, but as in radiant. "You're calling in a meditative practice and asking for support and guidance," they explained. "When I am regularly in my practice, I sit there and call in my support people. It just feels like this like warmth, and a big part of it is not feeling so isolated."

The animist practices Jazz has embraced center on love and worship of earthly beings and perceiving all things on this planet as beings. "So like a tree is not just a tree. It is a being," Jazz said. "It is a living being that communicates." Understanding that means you are never truly alone and fosters a sense of compassion and respect that goes beyond human form. It's a holistic view of the world and illuminates how connected we all are to the earth, to nature, and to everything. Creatures, plants, and places all possess a distinct spiritual essence.

Jazz basically identified as an atheist until two years ago, so embracing support from God or the spirit realm still feels somewhat foreign. "That's still an adjustment I'm making," they said. "But the reason why I stick with it and am willing to share about it is because the positive responses are so freaking palpable, especially the more diligently I practice." The past year has been especially difficult for Jazz, given racism, the coronavirus pandemic, and needing to move multiple times as a result. And they credit ancestral and animist practices for allowing them to survive. "I was just going through so much and having housing instability, and I'd lost really close friends earlier in the year," they said. "And I only felt like I could keep going because of [these practices]. And that's really a new experience."

To further heal their relationship with sexual pleasure, Jazz said they had to really "break it down" and consider that their body might be changed forever. "I had to think to myself, maybe you will never have pain-free sex again," they said, adding that they remained committed to seeking and embracing pleasure. While permanent vaginal pain and vaginismus symptoms didn't turn out to be the case for Jazz, that commitment would have remained a priority to them regardless. "I just really believe that pleasure is a birthright," they said. "I really, really believe that, for everyone. . . . So much of pleasure is in your brain. So unless you can't access your brain, then most everyone can really have quite a range of pleasurable experiences."

Jamila's Reflections

I want to offer that we don't need to worry about trying to get our lives *back*, but the more interesting and more powerful question of how am I going to live *now*? Often that is the very complex work: allowing our body to reveal the different levels of pain or unsafety that we've experienced. Complex as it may be, we need not do this alone. In truth, we are never really alone, even though so much of this culture tries to reinforce that you are either alone or you have to buy your support and wellness from within a consumerist mindset, that somehow you can free yourself from your past once you've bought all the right programs, attended all the best workshops, and all aspects of your life are completely balanced. This kind of "balance" is a fallacy.

And because we have a culture that's both consistently trauma-tizing and not yet completely trauma-informed, people often do feel very alone and almost alien. They feel lost for anyone who can safely hold their unique strangeness, meaning the shape of your life and its currents, the things that have influenced your particular journey.

Something else that struck me about Jazz's story was that they spoke of becoming acclimated to hard sex and enjoying the intensity of that, yet it was when they had a partner that touched them gently that they felt their body "close." I want to be very clear that it's abso-lutely OK to enjoy intense rough sex. It is not inherently a problem at all. Just as there are varieties of colors and sometimes we want pastels and other times we want vibrant bold jewel tones or even fluo-rescents, we can enjoy different kinds of sex. Or if we think of sex like food, what I want for you is to be able to enjoy a variety of food and feel nourished and satisfied each time you have a good meal.

So what does all this have to do with roughness? In my years as a sex educator and sex therapist, I've noticed that many of the folks will express that they are very comfortable with rough sex, but they're not comfortable having slower or soft sex. I've wondered if some people need that high intensity because we've been living in this kind of disconnected state in our bodies for so long in order to survive this culture, and only intense stimulation can break through that callous-ness and allow us to feel something. Again, there is nothing wrong with seeking a way out of disconnection and into fuller feeling, or having a brain style that craves rapid activity or can't easily or feasibly slow down. What I want for people is increased access to the variety of sensual and sexual pleasure that's available.

When we have been traumatized or society continues to perpetuate trauma and create unending harshness, softness and gentleness can sometimes feel like the most agitating, frightening, awful thing that we can experience. It can be much easier to have a hard fuck with some-body who may or may not care about you then to have somebody gently peer in your eyes and touch parts of your body with care, slowness, admiration, and intention. For many of us that can be almost unendur-able. As I said, please understand it's not a matter of trying to convince people to move from harder sex more often to having softer sex more often. Not at all. Play on and play loud, hard, or fast, as much as you want! But just as there are times when we gobble down food to quickly satiate hunger, there are times that call for savoring food longer, how-ever that looks for you. Given the relentless intensity we are having to survive every day, it's important to make sexual and sensual connection a ceremony or ritual or to slow down enough to taste every part of it. Slowing down allows us space. In that space, you can better under-stand how your body works in that moment and fine-tune where the pleasure lies for you. And if you have a "fast brain" due to neurodiver-gence, you can embrace active ways of slowing things down; slow does not have to equal long, static, and laborious. Give yourself the luxury of spaciousness to see what's really there so that you can find the words you might need, and so that, during partnered sex, your partner can see your reactions to your responses, learn your exhalations, movements, and expressions, and you can do the same for them so that you have even more to explore and more to build on as time goes by. Consider offering yourself the same during solo sex.

YOU ARE NOT TRULY ALONE

Although many of us carry pain, the way it shows up in our lives, how we are able to navigate it, and how others are able to support us can vary drastically from person to person. Too often, our wellness is tied to our past and current socioeconomic status. The internal sense of isolation and alienation that many of us have felt or may still feel haunts many of us. When it seems as though nobody in your world cares about you, I urge you to know in the deepest internal part of you that you are never, *ever* alone and you are never, *ever* unlovable.

What I hope you take from Jazz's story is that possibilities exist that go beyond the therapist's couch or talking with a friend, although both are incredibly important. Jazz's courage to begin practicing animism and ancestor worship illustrate deeply life-affirming methods for reminding ourselves how connected we actually are, to our bodies, to the world around us, to every ancestor that's come before us and those who will come after us. After decades of living within a culture that tends to center monotheistic religions and Christianity in particular, it can be an incredible paradigm shift for Black and/ or Indigenous and other people of color to embrace working with Indigenous- or African-inspired spiritual paradigms.

What I desire most for you is discovery of the paradigms that best help create internal coherence in your life. Practices help you cultivate an ethical moral center that helps you return to your body and navigate the world in ways that make you feel good and support your wellness and the wellness of other people. That wholeness can come from the practices of monotheistic traditions and from religious traditions that have pantheons of gods with animist traditions. All of these can provide paths of healing and right living.

Jazz is still in the beginnings of having confidence and trust in their spiritual practice and continuing to find that the more they deepen and consistently practice their awareness that they are interconnected with the spirits of the world around them, the more they're able to feel centered, connected, and less alone. Jazz is already experiencing the wellness that derives from a deep awareness of the ancestors and spirits of the world around us.

If you are beginning a new spiritual practice, it's completely understandable to feel a little silly, "crazy," or ridiculous. So many of us have endured disconnection from our ancestors. I've witnessed in my work and the larger world that no matter what the particular healing path looks like, the practices of connection, centering or grounding, listening to your body, giving of yourself in service to the community, and finding connection are commonalities. Whatever particular frame you're working from, these practices can lead you to the place where you want to be, a place of pleasure, integrity, and groundedness as you move through life. One of the greatest traumas for Black people and people of color, particularly Indigenous people, has been the physical death of too many of our people and the spiritual death or the destruction of our religious traditions. I don't think it can be understated how profoundly damaging the concerted efforts to destroy our linkages with religious traditions were and continue to be. When we are left without a spiritual and moral center, anything can take its place—especially things that are not truly nourishing. Into that moral and spiritual void will come people, places, and behaviors that aren't truly pleasurable, but that stoke the fire to get more and more, or they leave us stonehearted or callous toward other folks.

You do not have to be religious or claim a particular spiritual paradigm, but I do encourage people to cultivate mindfulness, intentionality, care, and compassion for themselves and for other people in their lives, and you can call all of that whatever you wish. Or, you can deepen the spiritual or religious paths that make the most sense to you. Many books and communities, online and off, can provide support and guidance to deepen your own spiritual practices. You need not spend large amounts of money in order to walk any kind of a spiritual path or learn more about a spiritual path that you're curious about. If people have your well-being and their own well-being in mind, any required monetary resources will be sustainable. Every religion and every spiritual practice has some parable, text, story, figure, practice, or elements about sensuality and pleasure, that centers on the body and sexuality as sacred. I don't know of any religion that does not have such a tradition somewhere within its paradigm. Find the one that speaks to your spirit, follow it, and experiment. See what joys and openings it creates for you.

Grounding Exercise

Close your eyes and imagine that you're a tree, standing strong and solid in an open pasture or forest, desert, or by the ocean. Take slow, deep breaths, stretching your arms like branches, if you wish. Imagine that you're breathing in the earth's energy as your roots connect with the soil beneath your feet. What do you notice in this place? Whom do you want to welcome into this inner world with you?

9

"Should I Forgive? If So, How?"

Forgiveness, run through me
Be a river shifting my silt, always changing
Make me a beautiful impermanence
—adrienne maree brown, "Forgiveness Litany"

In a conversation with poet Maya Angelou published in *Shabala Sun* in January 1998, author, professor, and social activist bell hooks said that for her, forgiveness and compassion are always linked: "How do we hold people accountable for wrongdoing and yet at the same time remain in touch with their humanity enough to believe in their capacity to be transformed?" This concept can feel complex. Some survivors feel compassion toward an abuser who was abused as well, seeing that they've been not only a perpetrator, but a victim. Other survivors believe there is no explanation that can come close to justifying holding compassion for such a person. You need not feel guilt or shame for taking either of these stances. Whether you feel compassion for a person who harmed you or not, your emotions and your take on forgiveness are valid.

It's also not uncommon to hear about forgiveness in the context of love. Do we need to love someone or condone their behavior in order to forgive them? Or is forgiveness really about letting someone or something go, so that we, ourselves, can experience freedom?

Given survivors' responses we received about forgiveness, it seems clear that whether or not you choose to forgive, as well as how helpful (or not) it can be, rests largely in how you define forgiveness in the first place. Many of the folks who choose not to forgive feel that forgiveness requires stating that a traumatic event, or series of events, were "OK" or at least not such a big deal. Many people who find forgiveness medicinal see it as a means not of justifying someone's behavior, but of moving on, for their own sake and perhaps for the people they love. Dictionary definitions tend to look at forgiveness as no longer feeling angry or resentful toward someone for a mistake or offense. The goal there could be both a lighter load and more pleasurable life for you, as well as, potentially, for the person or people who harmed you. There is a pleasure to be found by seeing forgiveness as something to resist because it seems to justify harmful behaviors. One can find a deep satisfaction that stems from standing your ground and never condoning that which isn't right. Pleasure is also possible when we hold seemingly contradictory emotions, such as anger for someone's harm and compassion for their own pain. Some people experience a deep contentment from giving themselves the grace and permission to experience both. And both scenarios can bring the pleasure that derives from taking care of yourself by making decisions that support and strengthen you.

Whether or not you prioritize forgiveness in your journey is *fully* up to you, and you have the right to change your mind or stance about it at any given time. You can even stay in an "I don't know" place, or where choosing whether or not to forgive isn't a priority at all. Only you can know what's ideal for you. If you feel stuck in these areas, consider sorting it all out with a trusted therapist, if possible.

In some cases, self-forgiveness is hugely important while managing trauma, even if you haven't done anything "wrong." The perception that you have may draw up a need to radically accept what happened, as well as your perceived involvement, so that you can more easily move on. If you harbor resentment or anger toward yourself, steering clear of forgiveness might feel as though you're somehow compensating, or as though that "punishment" helps matters somehow. In reality, you deserve the utmost self-compassion, especially if you feel unworthy of it. As a movement facilitator, somatics teacher and practitioner, and writer, Prentis Hemphill asserted in an essay called "On Healing," that healing requires "the capacity to deeply listen and a commitment to self-knowing." He then described self-knowing as a way of listening, one "where we ask ourselves questions and allow ourselves to wait for the answers . . . [and] allow the answers to be honest, even when they're disturbing or contradict the story we try to tell of who we are." Setting your sights on these two aims might help you navigate decisions around forgiveness while bolstering your healing process.

> How do you define forgiveness? Is cultivating forgiveness a priority for you? Why or why not?

CHERYL: OWNING HER STORY, FORGIVENESS AS FREEDOM

Cheryl Hunter grew up in an area of Colorado so rural that there were practically "no signs of civilization." If she climbed to the top of a tree and sort of craned her head, she said, she could see part of a freeway in the distance. And in many ways, she found the horse ranch she grew up on idyllic.

"I remember lying down in the meadow and looking up at the sky and seeing planes occasionally and thinking that if I stared hard enough at that plane," she remembers, "I could get sucked up inside of it and then I'd be the one in that plane looking down at this girl lying among the cow patties on the rough grass of the meadow." She longed to get out of the small town and explore the world. So one day, she decided to page through *Glamour* in hopes of finding career advice that would allow her to do precisely that. When she read about their need for models, she figured why not? She was tall enough to play on the boys' basketball team at the time, and what other prerequisite could there be? She could smile for long periods of time, no problem.

To fulfill her plan of becoming a model so she could live in a big city, Cheryl convinced a friend to join her on a grand adventure of a trip to Europe. Once Cheryl's mother reluctantly gave her the go-ahead, the pair saved up, boarded a plane, and headed to France. All the while, no one besides Cheryl knew about her modeling plans. Soon after arriving, a man wearing a camera around his neck approached Cheryl and asked her if she was a model. If not, he could *make* her one. Delighted that her plan was coming together so easily, Cheryl left her friend, who warned, "Oh, no you don't." But Cheryl was determined.

Rather than make her a model as he had promised, that man and another man drugged, beat, and raped Cheryl repeatedly over the course of several days. At one point, she entered one of those proverbial near-death experiences, where your whole life seems to flash before your eyes. She talked out loud about her brother, and how smart he was with his many ideas for inventions. And she spoke of her grandmother, who often wanted to hold her hand while they were out shopping. But Cheryl, feeling "too cool" for that as a teenager, would pull her hand away. Now she wished she'd held on.

Finally, the men dumped her in a park, leaving her for dead. As soon as she could find her way to a phone, Cheryl called her mother, but all she could utter was, "I'm OK . . . I'm OK . . . I'm OK." For more than a decade, Cheryl told no one about the attack, trying instead to disconnect from it as much as possible, trying to will it out of existence. Later, experts told Cheryl that speaking about her family likely humanized her to her captors in what was a trafficking attempt gone awry.

Cheryl did eventually cultivate a successful modeling career, which required a lot more than smiling for lengthy amounts of time as she'd predicted. By age twenty-three, she had lived in seven countries and was featured in every major magazine franchise and became the worldwide Coca-Cola girl. While she excelled, she was also in a career path that not only didn't encourage open or vulnerable conversation, but also essentially discouraged it. No one hires you to model because of your conversational capabilities.

Meanwhile, Cheryl struggled with depression, and the trauma of all that had happened to her in Paris distanced her from her loved ones. When she told her mother she was depressed, without mentioning possible reasons as to why, her mom misunderstood and thought that Cheryl was bored and suggested that she consider helping others. So Cheryl started volunteering in senior living facilities. There, she met Holocaust survivors who would shift her perspective.

"I got fascinated with their stories because there were some who had done beautifully with their lives," she said. "But there were some who, very understandably, were bitter and hard and resentful. And again, nobody could ever blame them." The more fascinated she became with their stories, the more questions she asked—and most were eager to answer. "I spent all of my time there," she said, adding "ultimately helping other people became my path out of hell." From the residents, she learned she wasn't alone in having survived trauma and that moving on to a place of thriving was possible.

In addition to volunteering with seniors, Cheryl began attending personal development programs to facilitate the next chapter in her healing journey. Eventually, after taking every available program she could find, she trained to lead the programs themselves. She found the rigorous training especially therapeutic. Eventually, she started giving seminars on a range of topics related to personal development. During one of those talks, she felt compelled to share her own story with trauma for the first time. A discussion ensued about forgiveness, something she had presented about in very hypothetical "it can be helpful" ways. Someone in the audience remarked that some happenings are so vile, that forgiveness isn't possible. And because, by Cheryl's definition, forgiveness involves setting yourself free and she believes it's accessible to almost anyone, she shared aloud the trauma she had been through for the first time. And she hasn't stopped speaking out or, her most valued work, raising the voices of other survivors since.

Playing a role in other people's healing has helped her to continue moving forward, Cheryl said, providing a sense of purpose and fulfillment while making way for more pleasure in her life. Throughout these experiences, she's learned that pleasure is a challenging area of life for many survivors, particularly for those who experienced signifiers of pleasure during a traumatic event, such as an orgasm during an assault. She's heard from many people who correlate the effects of trauma as some sort of punishment for the positive emotions or sensations they felt at the time. As a result, she sees many of these people "omitting basic self-care, whether it's the real necessities, not eating regularly, not sleeping, not getting enough exercise, or even water . . . let alone moving on to things like sexual pleasure and allowing themselves to orgasm."

Cheryl's relationship to pleasure has shifted over the years, too, and continues to be a work in progress. "Some of the things I see in myself in denying myself pleasure is not vacationing, often working too hard," she said. "I can see there's that 'punishment factor' that I still have to really keep in check, even though I would say that my healing journey in some regard is complete. I can see that punitive relationship with myself, like pushing myself hard and making myself work really hard and not taking breaks, etc. as if somehow punishment will right the order of things."

Cheryl has also worked through relationship strife related to trauma. For years, she had a strained relationship with her father, although they had been close during her childhood. Through therapy, Cheryl realized she felt upset and angry toward her father for not protecting her when she was attacked, even though he was on the other side of the globe at the time and she didn't tell him what happened for over a decade. For years after the kidnapping, all Cheryl was holding inside adversely affected her relationship with her father. "Once I actually spoke with him about what happened," she said, "it allowed both of us to process and heal. Since then, our relationship has been better than ever." It wasn't a onetime conversation, she added, and finally communicating honestly "created an opening for transparency in the relationship." Cheryl went on to say, "Each time we authentically share our truth, it creates a deeper connection with others. So ultimately, the attack has impacted my relationship with other people and the healing work I've done has allowed me to connect profoundly with them."

ANDREA: PLEASURE TO BEHOLD, FORGIVENESS AS OPTIONAL

If you do a web search about trauma, many articles and studies you find will mention how common it is to endure at least one traumatic experience at some point. What most of these publications fail to mention is the fact that many of us experience not one, but multiple or even serial traumas. In cases of emotional, physical, and sexual abuse, these crises are more often perpetual for some amount of time. If you can relate, know that you are not alone and that you are deeply worthy of healing, pleasure, and connection—even if pleasure feels daunting at times, or if there's still a great deal that you or a partner don't yet understand.

Andrea has had stomach issues since toddlerhood. While it's hard to say whether these issues are one hundred percent connected, they said, "It's also impossible to say they are *not* connected," given that the childhood sexual abuse they endured started before they turned two. Sexual abuse by a family friend was followed by years of multiple forms of abuse by their stepfather from ages five to nine, as well as abusive situations and partners in adulthood. Andrea's last partner before their current one regularly coerced them into sex.

"As a child, my stomach would swell due to acid production, becoming hard and red like a watermelon," they said, adding that they became nauseated any time they felt an intense emotion, such as anger, fear, or shame. By early elementary school, Andrea was engaging in self-injury behaviors that intensified over time. Both self-injury and psychiatric medications made the stomach problems worse and eventually landed Andrea in the hospital, when they couldn't even keep water down. Andrea has learned to manage "stomach attacks" through a combination of dietary changes and medicinal marijuana. Because their nervous system often perceives threats when there are none out of self-protection, Andrea also experiences panic attacks.

All of these trauma responses have impacted Andrea's intimate relationships, they said, many of which have ended because of their trauma history. Leading up to the breakups, Andrea has had difficulty communicating their needs. "I have had people leave because I was unable to meet their needs sexually," they said, "both through my trauma standing in the way and also their inability or unwillingness to approach sex with me in ways I needed." Rather than bring delight, excitement, or release, sexual pleasure has often invoked a fear response in Andrea, who added, "Through self-work, medication, and learning more about consent and boundaries, this has been minimized, but it still can happen if my mindset is not prepared."

In most of their romantic relationships, Andrea seemed to have less interest in sex, compared to their partners. In their current relationship, they realized that low libido is not the issue. Rather, the challenge has been that due to chronic boundary violations, Andrea had to learn and practice clearly stating and enforcing their boundaries. Thankfully, Andrea's current partner of four years seeks their consent about sexual acts. "Having someone who respects me enough to ask, continually and without fail, has shown me that having boundaries respected allows me to relax and have a healthy sex life with my partner," they said. "I also have realized that while I mostly dated men before, I think this was more out of thinking I was attracted to men instead of realizing I was attracted to masculinity. Dating men meant that I found myself often repeating abuse patterns. After entering a relationship with a butch woman, I am unsure I would date a cis-het man again at this point."

Inner child work that included support from a shamanic guide also had a profoundly positive impact on Andrea's healing journey. This work involves "rescuing" your inner child while you're in a meditative state. "A simple way to think of it is that your inner person shatters at each moment of intense trauma," they said. "You can go 'inside' and find them, where they are stuck at those moments. You do some shamanic work to 'cord cut' and then take them to a safe place." This process has allowed Andrea space between their wounded parts that are reacting as though the abuse is happening in the present, versus the past. "I can often feel the reactions that I would have had previously," they said, "but there is now space and those reactions don't feel like me anymore." This was one of the first modalities Andrea tried that said "you will never get over [the trauma], you should be angry and upset about it, but you can take action to move those wounded parts to a safe place so that they no longer run your life."

Andrea has also had varying degrees of success from talk therapy, medication, reiki, meditation, and kinesiology. After their last breakup, Andrea embraced several years of remaining single, including about two years of romantic and sexual celibacy, to focus on self-work. "I promised myself that I would not engage in those activities until I was one hundred percent sure I could enforce my boundaries, and promised myself that I would never again have sex that I didn't want to have," they said.

As a trauma-specializing sex therapist, Jamila has had a significant impact on how Andrea views pleasure—something that's long felt frightening. While they never worked together as therapist and client, after meeting Jamila and hearing her speak, Andrea said they can view pleasure as a way to say "fuck you" to the people who have hurt them. "It's not something that is scary to be used against me, but something healing to be used *by* me," they said. Pleasure can still feel triggering at times, Andrea said, but they now see it as something to value instead of something to suffer through out of fear.

Andrea wants fellow survivors to know that forgiving an abuser is not required, and that while such forgiveness is healing for some people, it is not helpful for everyone. "Forgiveness is often touted as the true path to healing, but the same people who tout forgiveness often want the current environment to remain, which allows abusers to not be held accountable," they said. "I often see forgiveness as maintaining that status quo, because if I forgive my abusers, the rest of society doesn't have to face that this happens *All. The. Time.* Don't let your anger and sadness consume you, but know you can hold onto those as power and strength. Your path is your own. Do what feels right, no matter what anyone else tells you." If you do so and refuse to give up, they added, lasting happiness is possible.

Forgiveness is a process, and we do not believe that you have to forgive somebody in order to move forward in your healing process or move on with your life. Coming to some sort of understanding about it is important, but forgiveness of the perpetrator, the person who harms you, is not necessary. When we think in terms of the larger systems such as racism, ableism, and class that harm people, forgiveness has no place. These structures don't care. They are not human. They just continue to harm people. So to speak about forgiving something when it's a system that by definition harms people has no true or active meaning. In that context, forgiveness is a dangerous idea because it locates the need to forgive within the person who has been harmed as though they can somehow move past barriers such as genderism, homophobia, or being denied economic opportunity. It implies that somehow not forgiving is what's causing harm, instead of the structures. Having an ongoing conversation with yourself, your therapist, or other loved ones about what forgiveness can look like for you is important. Equally important is knowing that forgiveness may or may not happen and that that is unique to your individual journey.

Grounding exercise

Picture the face or imagine the voice of someone you love. Imagine taking in all the encouragement and support you see in their eyes or hear in their words. Create a mental image of it: Is it a sound, a glow, a color? An object? Imagine really bringing this image closer to yourself.

10

"Dang. I Thought I Was Healed."

Jamila's Reflections

Healing is not a onetime event because life itself is not a onetime event. When you first hear that, you might feel upset, angry, sad, or hopeless. (If any of that is coming up right now, take your time to breathe, hug, or pat yourself and perhaps write about or record those feelings and thoughts.) Still, I'm thankful for the truth that healing is lasting and expansive. The profound lessons that we learn during our healing process will strengthen our capacity for compassion, intentionality, curiosity, joy, and, of course, pleasure. However, life's challenges and stressors don't stop just because we have made the decision to (re)claim our lives. It can be incredibly frustrating, if not outright enraging, to feel buffeted or ambushed by the vicissitudes of life and/or the impacts of structural discrimination/harm. I want to encourage you to push back against the trap of thinking that you are not doing enough to be healed, and push back against the idea that healing is a thing or a process that you can buy.

Healing is not something that comes solely from outside of you. There is nothing fundamentally wrong with you. You're in this process of trying to heal, and healing cannot be rushed. It takes the time it takes, and there is nothing that can accelerate it beyond its capacity at that time. So often, I'm trying to create metaphors for my clients that will help them live in this understanding. Such understanding is needed because this culture will tell you there's a definite way or that you need to "hurry up," that you can get to the end and then you'll be "normal," actualized, or superhuman. What I want to offer people is a slower and deeper paradigm that focuses on cultivating and noticing, and that prioritizes relationships with yourself and others. That is the only thing that I've seen that brings sustained individual change. On a larger scale, we need structures and programs in place that support process and relationship over time instead of hype, consumerism, and quick fixes.

I often use the metaphor of a broken bone or a medical condition when working with my clients. It's not so much that once we know the bone is broken, immediately it'll be healed and fixed. There's a longer process toward its healing that you have to tend to. You might need physical therapy, and your life now has to shift to accommodate this new challenge and this process of healing. Or if we have a chronic condition or disability, lifelong management, adaptations, and accommodations are needed and deserved. Emotional wounds function similarly, particularly wounds that are related to our relationships. When we've been wounded in a relational way, it is only through a new kind of relationship and a new kind of relating over time that we find and live our way toward wellness. Practices of pleasure are the way through that.

As a culture, we often confuse or have a limited idea of what pleasure is. I want to expand the idea of what pleasure is and highlight the tool and guide that it can be. Pleasure is not always something that, from beginning to end, makes us feel happy. If we look at pleasure in a more expansive way, pleasure can also mean contentment, satisfaction, quiet calmness, the fierce rush of internal movement toward coherence, or outward struggle against an adversary or challenge. Contained within each of these different phrases are possibilities for different ways to measure the work that we're doing. Often healing from trauma is challenging, difficult, scary, and exhausting. But these are the same kinds of emotions that happen anytime we do anything that's worth doing well.

When you're in school working on a project or goal, having a conflict with a partner or loved one, working toward a professional accomplishment, or when you're exercising and you feel your body reaching toward that next level, these challenges can involve pleasure too. There's also pleasure in learning new practices and leaning into our principles, but not the arrogant self-satisfaction of *I'm so much better than somebody else*. When we do the hard work of adhering to our principles or do what we know to be the right thing, when our ethics come into play, that, too, is its own kind of pleasure. When we're committed to healing, committed to growth, committed to connection, and committed to pleasure there can be a kind of pleasure in doing anything. In adhering to these commitments: *Even though I don't want to write, I am still going to write. I am going to exercise because I know I will feel good once I'm in the zone. I am going to say this challenging thing to myself or I'm going to speak these words to another, even though it feels like the hardest thing I've ever done, and is maybe the hardest thing I've ever done*. Pleasure can be found in doing *that thing* and putting voice to that experience, in reaching for something different and better than what you had before, and then in looking back and saying, *I did that*. Practicing pleasure in these ways will lead you where you want to go and us as a species to a deeper sense of interconnection.

People often come to psychotherapy not at the beginning of distress, but when they are at their wits' end. People are smart, and most folks will have tried a multitude of ways to survive, cope, and move forward. I am always in awe of someone's courage to seek out therapy, to enter into a new relationship with so many unknowns. No matter where you are in that journey, more healing and pleasure are available to you moving forward.

WINNIE: "BABY STEPS" BACK TO PLEASURE

Writer, activist, and researcher Winnie M. Li was working as a film producer in London when her life was disrupted by trauma. During a trip to Belfast, the day before a red-carpet event for a feature film she had worked on, she decided to engage in one of her greatest passions: spending time alone in nature. About ten minutes into what should have been a restorative hike, a teenage boy approached her for directions.

"I'm Chinese American, and if you hear me, I obviously sound American. So I thought it was strange when he was asking me for directions when I clearly wasn't from Belfast," she remembered. "And I guess he sort of used that to start talking to me. . . . I had one of those weird conversations, where I don't know why this person is talking to me. So after about ten minutes, I said, 'I've got to make a phone call to a friend'—something any of us would try to do. I called a friend and didn't really have any reception at the time. But I was really out there to hike, so I just kept on going on the trail, and little to my knowledge, he was following me."

Once Winnie reached a secluded area, the boy assaulted her so violently, she was left with thirty-nine separate injuries. She recalls experiencing flight, fight, and freeze throughout the attack. At first, she fought and attempted to rush away, but quickly realized she was dealing with a very violent person who could end up causing her brain damage or killing her if she kept resisting. So at a certain point, she decided to succumb to his demands.

"It's a strange thing," she said. "Other victims of sexual violence might relate to this experience. Once you sort of give in to whatever this person is asking for, it doesn't become as physically dangerous. So it becomes a survival decision. It's *always* a survival decision. That's why it always angers me when people say, 'Well why didn't you do this or this?' Well your brain is assessing what to do to stay alive."

After the attack, Winnie reached a friend by phone, who offered the support she needed: believing Winnie and helping arrange logistics for the next steps. After police reports and care at the hospital, media outlets caught wind of the attack, spurring a frenzy of headlines: "Chinese tourist raped by a teenage boy." At one point, Winnie heard her case being discussed on a hugely popular radio program. "There actually was a woman who called up and said, 'My heart goes out to that Chinese girl, because her life is now ruined,'" she reflected. "And I remember hearing that and thinking, "That's kind of weird. . . . There's almost an assumption that I'm going to be living the rest of my life in shame."

For a solid year after the rape, Winnie's life was on hold, as though she would try to take one step forward and fall several steps back. For a while, she feared she would never return to her previous self. Winnie before the assault was very outgoing, confident, and loved traveling on her own. Now she could barely leave her own apartment due to crippling agoraphobia.

"I was getting flashbacks and panic attacks all the time, so I just felt so diminished as a person," she added. "I often describe it as you're a fish that's been gutted. So maybe on the outside I seemed fine, but on the inside I was completely hollow [and] couldn't feel emotions properly. I just didn't have the self-confidence. I was just a ghost of the person I was before. And there was a great sense of loss, because I was wondering, 'Did this fifteen-year-old boy take everything away from me?' And oftentimes it felt like that. But eventually, over time, I did recover."

Some of Winnie's healing process came by way of baby steps toward reconnecting with the confident, nature-loving version of herself she recalled and missed. Determined to shift the outdoors from a major trigger to something she could freely enjoy again, she asked herself if she could manage five minutes on her own at a park, and started there. Once she could manage that, she aimed for fifteen minutes, describing the process as "pushing myself a little bit in the direction of what I used to love doing, and eventually being able to reclaim it that way."

There were many times through her healing journey that Winnie felt the "opposite of brave," she said. Finally, though, after many steps, such as visits to a local park and talking to strangers, she booked a round-trip ticket to Southeast Asia, where she would backpack for three months. "I realized that the majority of people in this world are good people," she said. "As a Chinese person, I don't stick out [in Southeast Asia], so I blended in a fair amount and maybe felt safer that way. . . . So I did that and it was amazing and nothing bad happened to me."

While Winnie realizes that not everyone wishes or needs to speak about their experience as a victim or survivor of sexual violence, Winnie felt compelled to. So often we only hear about a survivor's worst moments, she said, which can be pretty dehumanizing. Her own story had been discussed around the world. "If anyone has the right to tell that story, it's me," she decided. "It's the survivor. . . . Storytelling is my thing, so I'm going to use my skills to tell my story on my own terms."

Once she felt ready, she did just that, completing a novel based on her experience called *Dark Chapter* that would go on to be released around the world in various languages, including German, Swedish, Dutch, Italian, and Chinese, and garner awards and nominations, such as the Guardian's Not the Booker prize in 2017 and a nomination for best first novel in the prestigious Edgar Awards in 2018. It's written from two fictionalized perspectives: a young woman who was raped as Winnie was and the teenage rapist. She also launched the Clear Lines Festival, the UK's first-ever festival dedicated to addressing sexual assault, abuse, and consent.

People often ask Winnie if she forgives her attacker, who ended up getting convicted with a sentence of eight years, of which he served half. "I'm not there," she said. "Some people do feel the need to [forgive], but I wrote the book, and the act of writing him in a book, imagining him as a human being—there is some empathy for the perpetrator at some point. I was trying to figure out how someone would evolve into a rapist at such a young age. To me, that's similar to forgiving him, I suppose . . . someone who has the ability to rehabilitate."

Jamila's Reflections

Winnie spoke of feeling hollow and gutted. That deeply somatic, visceral feeling is common when we've had acute trauma or been living under many onslaughts to our sense of self. We may have this chronic feeling of hollowness or as though our emotional responses don't sync up with the rest of the world. This feeling of "strangeness" and profound isolation can become a secondary trauma. Sometimes the depth or chronic nature of trauma is so profound, it can sort of short-circuit our ability to feel anything at all.

If you're experiencing these feelings, I invite you to take a breath, hug, progressively squeeze or stretch your body, and think about your body. Think about your chest or your throat or stomach or shoulders. Can you feel a kind of numbness, coldness, agitation, pain that's there all the time? It can be so omnipresent that we seldom even notice it anymore. That's not bad. It's merely information that tells us that right now, this is how your body is protecting you. This is how your body has tried to protect you. And all we want to do in each moment is notice and pay attention to the hollow, gutted feeling. Some of my other clients have mentioned feeling like a cold wind is blowing through their chest all the time. Find your own images, your own metaphors, your own language for what you experience in your body in this moment or in other moments when you can.

BRAVERY AS FEAR PLUS ACTION

Media and movies are saturated with depictions of bravery in the United States and other cultures. Standing stalwart in the field. Approaching a person that wronged you and giving them some clear, concise put-down. Getting a gun and shooting at somebody. I want to challenge these very onetime kinds of images of what bravery supposedly looks like. I fundamentally feel that bravery is fear plus action.

And sometimes bravery is fear plus exhaustion plus action. One can be so tired or fearful of having to live a certain way for the rest of their life that there's enough fear, desperation, rage, or tiredness to finally want to do something different. And so bravery is not these onetime events, nor does it always look pretty or strong. It may look vulnerable and transparent. Bravery can function almost like a volcano, something erupting inside, to generate even just one word. It often involves a quavering voice, shaking knees, or sometimes feeling nauseated. And then, the courageous move is slightly easier or different the next time.

Anybody who is reading this book, who has gone to therapy, who is trying different ways to move through their trauma because they just couldn't stand it anymore, is showing bravery. You're not just thinking about getting rid of something, but of trying to create a new life for yourself. That is some of the most profound courage that I could ever think of. So please be compassionate with yourself about how long the process seems to be taking.

Winnie found healing through following her pleasure. She remembered how going outside brought her bliss, and she was not going to let that be stolen from her forever. And so she started with very small increments and built up from there, beginning with what used to bring her pleasure and joy. One thing that's so profound about Winnie's story was that her reclamation occurred through her writing, her ability to not to escape what happened and put words to her experience. Her writing was her way of documenting her process, of creating something new, and of understanding and then sharing her experience. That is so critical, and it doesn't need to be a book. You can write a letter or postcard, scribble in a notebook, jot words down on a computer document or in an email to yourself on your phone. Writing your memories, writing your reflections, writing your rage, writing your pain and your hopes, getting all of that out can be an invaluable part of your journey.

Winnie also speaks of empathy versus forgiveness. Empathy is not forgiveness. Empathy is understanding a person's context and worldview to the point where you understand why they would act the way that they did. Asking why they do what they do is not absolution. It is not forgiveness. It is not saying it's OK. It is getting metaphorically inside somebody else's world to see and be able to understand from their perspective how they came to behave a particular way. Empathy is not always easy, although I think it can be of powerful use in the world, and it can be a good practice when I work with clients who have challenging relationships with parents or loved ones. I encourage them to listen and try to understand the conflicts and better understand the complexity from the other person's perspective. I call that the story behind the story: why is this person acting in this way? It's not attempting to make them behave differently, but to understand their view. It's aiming to understand their story of why they interact in the ways they have. In this way, empathy can be a very powerful tool for moving through something, moving away from somebody else's view of you. If you understand that what they say or do is because the world influenced them in a particular way, then you can see that, even though you might be deeply impacted, it's not that you are bad or deserving of the harmful thing that happened or continues to happen.

With awareness of the context that's generated your suffering, you may be better able to understand that an entire system needs to be dismantled or replaced—versus saying to yourself, *Oh, this thing happened to me because I did X, Y, and Z* or *because I am this kind of person*. Empathy is literally locating what occurred or what is happening in the context outside yourself, and it can be very freeing to understand that these are the reasons behind the circumstances: *I am part of the circumstances, but I am not the cause of these things happening*. For these reasons, empathy can be a very profound practice.

BRIAN: PERMISSION TO STRUGGLE AND GROW

Brian R. Johns is a singer, songwriter, actor, and author with many stories to tell, including that of his own journey with trauma. During his early childhood, he was molested by a male family member. While he feared telling anyone about what happened at the time, it soon found light after a cousin revealed that he had been sexually abused by the same relative. At that point, Brian's parents enrolled him in counseling. Looking back, he's grateful that these conversations, both with his parents and a therapist, started early. "Being able to talk candidly about my experiences, past and present, with people who love and care about me has been the most helpful," he said.

Over the years, numerous aspects of sex and intimacy have felt triggering because of his trauma history. "I've never wanted to feel absolutely powerless during sex," he said, adding that he realizes that the sense of being controlled in a safe environment appeals to some people. "I always aim to make sure the other person is comfortable because I never want to impose on my partner." At times, Brian has felt he should have been more assertive in the bedroom, but instead held back for fear of making someone else uneasy in any way, a state he knows too well. And as with many survivors, particular words can be activating for him. "Whenever I've met someone with the same name as my abuser, I can't bring myself to date the guy, no matter how great of a person he is," he noted. Being sexually abused by a man complicated the ways he's felt about his bisexuality and how freely he could accept it too. "I felt like I was cheated out of discovering my sexuality on my own terms," he said. "Because of this, I looked at my same-sex attraction through the lens of my abuse." Lately, though, Brian has made the decision to proactively "divest from those feelings of powerlessness," guiding with this discovery: "I wasn't cheated out of loving myself authentically and embracing who I've come to be, and I'd rather live in that reality."

Throughout his adulthood, Brian has found communicating openly and honestly about sex with supportive friends or others who have endured sexual abuse to be both liberating and rewarding, he said. Doing so has allowed him to discover, feel, and know that he's not alone and to be heard without judgment. Feeling accepted and understood has chipped away at any sense of isolation and helped bolster his sense of self-worth.

Given that boys and men are less likely to disclose sexual assault compared to girls because of societal notions that being abused some-how detracts from one's masculinity, Brian implores men to continue to work on learning to love and accept themselves "on purpose." "This isn't the easiest journey to begin, but counseling and therapy are always viable sources of getting to a place of self-love and happiness," he said. " It's also imperative to understand that you don't have to adhere to the societal norms placed on masculinity. You really can define your own life, literally." He cautioned that stepping more fully into your authentic self rather than attempting to stifle your wounds or vulnerabilities might be met by undesirable opinions of others. But in short, those aren't your people. "I've learned that those who truly love you—outside of their own expectations for your life—will be there to support you through any choice you make," he said. "Love will stay."

Brian found more purpose and helpful expression in creating his book, *Ant in an Eggshell: The Fragile Fortitude of a Black Man*. The collection of poetry, proverbs, and "therapy sessions" that chronicles his healing journey after sexual abuse is especially meaningful, considering the pressures he's noted on Black men in particular to remain "strong, unmoving, [and] unfeeling." Early in the book, in a poem entitled, "Superficial," he wrote, "Men different and alike, despite being black, brown, red or white; change the superficial to cope with life."

If you find yourself in a place of frustration because pain you thought you had moved past crops up again, a trigger flare just when you thought you'd risen above, he encourages you to realize that trauma and healing have their own personalities. "Frustration is a signal to go deeper and aggregate the places that may have been covered up with poor coping mechanisms," he's learned. "Don't allow the pain to debilitate your will to reach for the life you deserve. If you desire great mental, emotional, and spiritual health, lean in the direction of self-care." That choice may not always feel ideal, and "manifest as some of the hardest conversations you've had or some of the most lonely nights," he said, "but on the other side of that discomfort is a peace that surpasses all understanding."

Jamila's Reflections

One of the many critical themes running through Brian's story and experiences are the threads of connection, community, and relationship. Brian has sought out and cultivated people who would allow him to be who he was with his trauma, to listen to what he had experienced, and to find people who would also be slow, tender, and careful with him, just as he was seeking to be slow, tender, and careful with them. It cannot be overstated how critical it is to have community around us. And once we do, the goal is to then shift, bit by bit, culture and society itself until we have a world where certain things that were so harmful to some of us when we were isolated are no longer normalized.

Brian's story also speaks to the rampant biphobia in many cultures, as well as these outdated and unhealthy damaging ideas of what masculinity is, as though masculinity cannot be soft or receptive or tender. His honesty about his own internalized shame around his sexual orientation and his interests is a really beautiful and vulnerable admission. None of us have escaped this culture. None of us have escaped internalized ideas about Blackness, about thinness, about ability, about social status, about money. There are so many parts of the psyche that this culture has infected. The work is not to pretend that these things haven't affected us or aren't inside of us, or to act as though we're *so much better* than other folks. The work involves remembering where we were, that we can always do better, and to support other people to do better as well. It's also learning to be softer, slower, more curious, and more tender, and all of this is done through relationship.

Although all of us are more than just our ethnicity, Black and Brown people in particular cannot afford to ignore the impact that racist culture has on our psyche, our psychological health, our emotional health, and our physical health. Nor can we afford to ignore the stories that are told about us, and, sometimes within our own cultures, perpetuated about us: stories about how women are supposed to be or how men are supposed to be, what are the qualities and attitudes that make a man or make a woman either legitimate or not worthy of care and protection or not worthy of love. Stories about having to match up to gender binaries to begin with. Brian's story also serves as a powerful testament to a commitment to practice tenderness and not needing to buckle under the narratives that are told about how a man is expected to behave sexually or how a Black man is supposed to live and love.

It is never easy to overthrow or extricate ourselves from the narratives that seem like they are bred into our blood and bones, and yet if we do not do that work, if we do not find other people to support us in that work, and if we do not support others in doing that work, then there is no liberation. There is no actual safety or wellness for you or for anybody else. Individual health is not wellness. We are only truly as healthy as the society in which we live and, if nothing else, this book is a challenge and an invitation to cultivate your pleasure as an act of resistance, as an act of creativity, as an active liberation and revolution, because you deserve that. I deserve that. And everybody that you come in contact with, even people that you will never meet in this life, deserve that.

If you love and are loved by a man or masculine-of-center person, have conversations with them about what they've learned about what it means to be masculine. Co-create new ways for their masculinity to express itself and have experiences of nurturing and tender masculinity that has power without having to be domineering, a masculinity that can be quiet and that can hold.

I understand that for some of us, men and masculinity are frightening, repulsive, terrifying, or symbolize nothing good because of past or ongoing experience fueled by damaging messages, and I will not take that away from you. I simply ask, are there alternatives? Can we cultivate something different in the future? If any of us are ever to survive our traumas or to thrive in spite of our traumas, it must always be couched within an expectation and a hope and a determination that the world can change for the better. That our bodies can feel different, that our relationships can feel different, that when we leave our homes, maybe not in two years or five years or ten years or before the end of our lives, we can walk out into safety. A healthier, more connected world is worth striving for.

> Take some time—a few moments, a few minutes, or even a few hours or the better part of a day as you're moving about your tasks—to imagine a safer, healthier, and more connected world. What would that look like for you? Or for a loved one? How about for a stranger?

Afterword
Our Process with This Book

August: Where should we start? At the beginning? [mutual laughter] How did you feel coming onboard for this initially?

Jamila: What's the right word . . . I was curious, but very wary because I was just coming away from that harmful situation with a White woman sex educator. And although you and I had had that really pleasant interaction for your podcast, even then I was very guarded. I enjoyed myself that day, but I knew that I was coming into the recording session in this guarded way. And so when I heard from you months later, I was kind of surprised. I thought, *Oh, that's really nice*, but I still felt wary the whole way through. With the invitation to write the foreword, I was very pleased. I thought, *Well, that's really sweet and like lovely. And I do believe in what you're doing. So I'm happy to do that.* And then with the offer to actually write the whole book together, again, I was intrigued and also wary.

August: I knew it was a big ask, but I didn't know how big of an ask, given what you'd been going through. I remember sitting in the studio during that recording and listening to the ways you were articulating managing trauma, and it was all very impactful. Initially, I thought I would do what I usually do and interview lots of different experts.

Then as you were speaking, it was so surreal to me. I kept thinking, "This is what the book needs. This is what readers need." And so I knew that you penning the foreword would be amazing. I was so grateful when you agreed to it.

Then as I was doing more research for the proposal, I kept going back to your words. I could hear you speaking. I got really excited and immediately wondered if I would seem overwhelming if I was like, "Hello! I know you barely know me, but would you like to write this book with me?" I remember telling a good friend of mine that I was so excited about the possibility of collaborating with you. I was trying not to get my hopes up too high. I would have completely understood if you weren't interested, and yet my heart was invested in the idea. So it meant so much, and continues to, that you've been willing and trusting enough to take a chance on this journey together. I also deeply appreciated that during our first conversation about the book, you shared a bit about the challenging experiences you were still dealing with at the hands of a White woman.

Jamila: Yes. Because of my own personal work, I knew that I needed to tell you where I was coming from. And it was also in some ways a first kind of bid for professional safety. I thought, *This does seem interesting, but this is a White woman whom I don't know very well. If anything is going to be possible, I have to tell her where I am in this moment. And then we'll see.* And that felt vulnerable but also powerful, and powerful in a way that years ago I wanted to learn how to be. Not harsh, and like, *You have to hit the mark. You have to be perfect in the ways I want you to be*, which has been, because of my own stuff, how I usually have come to power. But that's not a way to live. And so I wondered, how do I talk to this person from my vulnerability? I said to myself, if this isn't safe, *if you can't tolerate what I need and what's happening for me, then it absolutely is a no*. And when I shared, you were really wonderful about it. Which of course made me feel like, *Oh my gosh, OK. She seems like she could hold this complexity . . . shit.*

August: I so appreciate that contrast of *yay!* and *shit*. When we get something that we're hoping for, but part of us feels like, *I don't know if I actually wanted to hope for this!*

Jamila: Yes, and I'm curious about your personal and professional journey with that—when we get the outcome we were hoping for and that's somehow even more frightening or frightening in its own way.

August: That's a really good point. I'd never really cowritten anything really. I'd collaborated on creative projects, but never something as massive as a book. I'd heard about people who cowrite novels, for example, and thought, *How? You have two different brains!* If someone had asked me a year ago if I could see myself cowriting a book, I don't think that I would have said, "Yeah, totally." But with you and this book, it's felt very natural.

Jamila: And what allowed you to move into being open to and wanting to cowrite, as opposed to weaving in a variety of experts? What made that possible?

August: Your willingness to be vulnerable and forthright about your concerns, and your trust and openness along the way have made it possible. This book also feels deeply personal. We are speaking to people who are potentially navigating the darkest feelings they've ever experienced and exploring intimate topics that are so often stigmatized. And because you approach your work from your best expertise and personal experience, you know so well what it's like to go through these experiences.

I also knew you would bring insights that I couldn't provide in ways a collection of clinicians couldn't. It's sort of like the difference between walking into a crowded room of experts for bits of advice, versus having a heart-to-heart with a trusted professional in a private space. That's important, because I think readers will bring their most vulnerable selves to this process.

I think we complement each other well, too, as far as skills and shared values, around matters such as needing this book to be inclusive and illuminate the dark side of the self-help industry. And our voices seem to weave together well. I think we've been able to create a unified voice, in addition to our own unique voices. I feel like we got lucky there.

Jamila: Yes, as you said, trying to cowrite a manuscript with two different brains and two different personalities can be complex. And the fact that it then grew into this unified voice, you can hope for, but not predict, that kind of alchemy. I didn't know that it would happen. That's been this incredibly delightful surprise.

Another thing that strikes me is you know, here we are. We wrote this book. We started it just before the pandemic really hit. And I think it's still hard to grapple with what it means to try to write a book like this in the middle of a pandemic, in the United States, and when really everything we're talking about has become so crystal clear for so many people like this. All of our wonderful people who've told their stories did so during the pandemic. And together, I've kept realizing, *we're doing it!*

August: Yes! I remember we were supposed to have our celebratory, moving-forward-with-the-book brunch on a rooftop a day or two after the lockdown went into place in Los Angeles. Instead, we ended up raising a glass by text. It may take time for us to really grasp what it's meant to complete this work at this specific time. Our conversations and the people who've trusted us with their stories have kept me going. This whole process has inspired me to think more about community in my own life, and of course, pleasure.

Jamila: Yes, pleasure. Always going back to pleasure. It's fascinating to me that I have had to remind myself to prioritize pleasure at many points during this process, in which we are writing a book that encourages that very thing. The fact that it's been challenging for us to stay focused on pleasure while writing about pleasure shows how difficult doing so can feel in the culture and world we live in.

August: That's so true. I remember early on you noticed that we were talking a lot about trauma, but not very much about pleasure. That really shifted things for me. And we joked about donning our "pleasure glasses" whenever we wrote. I picture them as these glowing frames with rainbows beaming from out of them. [mutual laughs] I'm also really grateful that Kara has been so wonderful to work with as an editor.

Jamila: Yes, Kara has been fabulous and supportive. And yet again, I had to process *OK, now I'm working with two White women*—while at the same time, seeing how White women can be so problematic.

August: I don't think Kara or I would have blamed you if you weren't up for this for that reason. We see those problems, and I know we're always learning and make mistakes. I remember Kara saying, "Jamila, you are not responsible for being the Black sensitivity reader for this book."

Jamila: I remember that too. It meant a great deal and I was grateful. But then, again, once we feel safe, that's often when harmful or traumatic things happen. So there was this mix of relief and fear at the same time.

August: That's so understandable.

Jamila: She was receptive about changing the title too. First nasty one's son stole our first title, *Triggered*. But that turned out to be positive, in a way, because it helped lead us here.

August: I've been thinking about the naysayers, and even the trolls, we'll likely hear from at some point. On one hand, I think hearing from trolls will be a positive sign that we're having an impact. We aren't writing this book to avoid ruffling feathers. We want to challenge people—of course for the greater good. And anyone who feels defensive or like spouting out at us, I want to ask, "What is it about this work that feels so off-putting or offensive to you? Where does that come from?" Because, almost certainly, it has little to do with us.

Jamila: Here we are talking about being triggered. And here we are talking about pleasure. And in this culture, I feel like we're going to get shot from multiple sides, you know? Not both sides, but literally multiple sides, including from people that we would have thought would have supported this book. As a therapist, I'm nervous about other clinicians finding this ridiculous or absurd—or worse, damaging or dangerous. That kind of professional censure is there. I'm still relatively young in my career and also, I am speaking about these things, because I know them from my experience. I know them from the work that I've done, from things you've said and other people have said, and so part of me is like, "Well, if you don't think that this works, where were you? Why are you not thinking about this, more established people?" But I do feel vulnerable around that. And is this coherent? If I am going to take on certain constructs, is my stuff tight? We created something, knowing that it's imperfect. We don't have absolute access data or ten research assistants. We have followed our pain, followed our pleasure, and created something. I'm not prepared for the trolls. I don't know what it's like when people come out of the woodwork to just crap on your stuff. So I imagine that will sting.

August: Yes. If it's somebody else's book, it's easy to say, there is no one book for everyone. And trolls, be damned! When it's your own book, both are harder. I thought I was prepared for professional harsh reviews before my first book's release, given my careers—modeling, acting, and writing—involve somewhere around ninety percent rejection. But then I received a tough one and it really threw me. I recommend giving yourself permission to not read reviews when you feel more vulnerable, or at least avoiding reading them before bed.

Jamila: I love that we can ask for what we need, from friends or colleagues from whom we want certain kinds of feedback. And that we can scaffold the support, you and the critiques that we're seeking. And I think, honestly, August, one of the hardest and most beautiful gifts about this work has been folding ourselves into it. This book, for me, has clarified what I believe and what I need, as an individual. And in a really beautiful way, it's set a standard of like, "Oh, I get to ask for scaffolding and I get to ask for compassion. And I get to ask for support. And it's important for me to practice pleasure." I, too, am part of this process and this experience. And that feels really nice, to not be on the outside of something. The mental health field, in its most rigid forms, constructs therapists as outside of the process. And the best kind of clinical theories or paradigms are like, "No, you are changed as you change the other." And so we're daring ourselves to do that.

August: That image of folding ourselves in really resonates with me because certainly pleasure and community, which you and this process have taught me so much about, and really seeking that support and redefining pleasure—that it doesn't have to look a certain way. The seemingly "small" steps can be very powerful. I've found myself being a student of this book as we write it, which is pretty profound.

Jamila: Yes, a student of this book. We created this experience with the mindset that we're all students and teachers. I'm really interested in people's variations. That's really what I want to hear. Like, "Oh, I took this idea from this book and then here are the mantras that I created." I can't wait to see what variations on this music people create.

August: Yes, so exciting. I also find it interesting that a book manuscript takes such massive effort. Then when you're finished and submit it, it's this very quiet moment. One little press of "send." No confetti falls out of the sky. Nobody brought a cake, unless you ordered it, which is why I think it's important to celebrate. Now that we're nearing that point, have you thought about that?

Jamila: Because of my own continuing battle with perfectionism, there is only the next thing you have to do. You finish and then you're on to the next thing. So this process with you has been not even a reminder, but literally an awakening to, "Hey, Jamila. Did you know you could celebrate?" And the fact that you've held that space and ask this question is this beautiful shock to me. *I could celebrate this? Me?*

August: No wonder celebrating along the way isn't a given, if that's how the world operates. We celebrate a wedding or having a baby like it's the most exciting thing on the planet. And yes, those things can be incredibly exciting for a lot of people. But what about when you birthed a book? Or get your therapy license? I'm reminded of Jazz, in our book, and what they said about being in nature and—I have chills again—feeling that you are not alone in your most seemingly isolated times. If you really open yourself, you can feel solace from the trees and nature. So I think spending time outdoors might be part of my celebration, besides cake, which will probably always be a part of my celebrations.

Jamila: There will be something yummy. A tart. I'm not really a cake person, but I love fruit tarts because they're so colorful and have all these textures. So I think maybe a selection of tiny tarts will be part of mine. And of course, sparkling wine.

August: Yes, sparkling wine. Cheers to that.

Jamila: Yes, cheers.

Acknowledgments

JAMILA DAWSON

On my father's side I am granddaughter of Ollie, great-granddaughter of Ira. On my mother's side I am daughter of JoAnn, granddaughter of Lillian, great-granddaughter of Hallie. I name them because I would not be here but for the creativity and tenacity of these incredible Black women. I give thanks to the people whose bodies of work touch my heart, ground my body, and elevate my mind. Thank you, Zora Neale Hurston, Pauli Murray, Audre Lorde, bell hooks, and adrienne maree brown. You are my "intellectual aunties." To my parents, William and JoAnn Dawson, and to my brother, Khalid Dawson, I love you so much; the foundation of who I am comes from what you have taught me! I also offer gratitude to the authors and stories that allowed me to live in fiction when, for years, my reality was only desolation and pain. Shout out to *The* Polycule and my chosen family S.G. & E.K.E., who give me support, love, and great cocktails! To my sex educator community, my ethical non-monogamy community, and especially to my Leather community, I have only admiration for you. You create new worlds by your dedication to expansive sexuality, your ethics, and your unbridled enjoyment of pleasure. I'm thankful for my former therapist, my brilliant colleagues, and my amazing clients who allow me to be in relationship with them and who surprise, delight, and inspire me to keep doing this work. Many thanks to Jill Marr, our agent who found this project a home. Huge thanks to my and August's editor-extraordinaire, Kara Rota: your enthusiastic support from the jump and the whole team at Chicago Review Press made this dream real! And finally, to August; I cannot truly put into words how fun and *healing* it has been to work on this book with you. I am profoundly changed by your empathy, talented writing, courage, compassion, and unwavering support.

AUGUST MCLAUGHLIN

I'm profoundly grateful to my partner, Mike, my animal coworkers, my parents, my siblings, and my dearest friends for their ongoing love, care, and support. You fuel me. Thank you to our wonderful agent, Jill Marr; our editor, Kara Rota; and the whole team at Chicago Review Press, for believing in this book and our mission and helping us bring it into the world.

Thank you, thank you, thank you, every person who opened their heart to speak about their own experiences with pleasure, relationships, and trauma for the sake of this book. It would not have been possible without your trust, might, and wisdom. Thank you for sharing your hearts and experiences so we all may learn.

Above all, thank you, Jamila Dawson, for joining me in this wild, wonderful, challenging, and strengthening journey. I could never have accomplished anything close to what we have created without your trust, powerful sensitivity, and brilliance. I am so proud of us. May we always wear our pleasure glasses.

Appendix

Suggested Exercises and Illustrations

Visual exercises and prompts can be helpful tools as we manage trauma and cultivate and prioritize pleasure in our lives. Feel free to use the following exercises and illustrations to display in your home, save as screenshots on your desktop, or share on social media.

PLEASURE, SUPPORT, AND PERSONAL GROWTH

Every step you take toward building community, seeking worthy support, cultivating healthy relationships, and prioritizing pleasure in your life makes a valuable difference. Create a list of action steps you can take regularly, no matter how small or sizable, toward these things. Pull from the following list or create your own, allowing it to change and expand along with you:

- Ask someone you trust for help with a difficult task.
- Bake or cook soothing food.
- Call, text, or email a loved one when you could use comfort or support.
- Color or draw.
- Create a pleasure ritual.
- Create a pleasure-centric space in your home, using soothing items you already own.
- Cuddle with a loved one (pets count!).
- Dance.

- Drink water or another hydrating beverage.
- Join a support group.
- Journal about your feelings.
- Learn about and prioritize healthy sleep habits.
- Let yourself cry.
- Listen to music.
- Masturbate.
- Meditate.
- Move your body.
- Pursue a curiosity or passion.
- Read about a type of oppression you're not well versed in.
- Rest, actively or statically.
- Schedule time for your own personal pleasure.
- Smell your favorite aromas, such as a flower, spice, or food you love.
- Spend time with animals.
- Take a few slow deep breaths. Set reminders on your phone, if it helps.
- Take a social media break.
- Take a warm bath or shower.
- Take any needed medication.
- Try or review the grounding exercises in this book.
- Turn unnecessary phone alerts off.
- Try "tapping" (Emotional Freedom Technique), guiding yourself with a YouTube video.
- Volunteer in a way that feels nourishing.

MANTRAS FOR AN ACTIVATED FLARE

Repetition of soothing sounds or words can be extremely helpful in the aftermath of a panic attack or when we've been activated. Here are some phrases you can use to ground yourself back into the present moment:

> *In this moment, I am safe.*
>
> *Even though I'm frightened (angry, scared, feeling hopeless), I will get through this.*
>
> *These feelings are only temporary.*
>
> *I can breathe in, I can breathe out. I have my breath.*
>
> *I am not alone.*

We absolutely encourage you to create your own using language that feels true to you in this moment.

HOW CAN WE GO FROM TRAUMA RESPONSE TOWARD EROTIC/RESILIENT RESPONSE? BE WITH THE BODY.

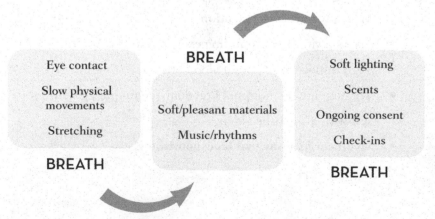

BREATH

Eye contact

Slow physical movements

Stretching

BREATH

Soft/pleasant materials

Music/rhythms

Soft lighting

Scents

Ongoing consent

Check-ins

BREATH

THE HEALING JOURNEY

<u>Trauma/Fragmentation</u>		<u>Wholeness/Integration</u>
Distress		Creativity
Dissociation		Pleasure
Fragmentation	➡	Expansion
Shame		Sharing
Isolation		Connection

Nb. Wellness is not binary; there are areas of wellness and areas of challenge/trauma for almost everyone.

WAYS TO NAVIGATE WITH A PARTNER

- Practice and integrate *interdependent* wellness.
- Do not go through this alone. (Get communal and/or psychological assistance. Create and maintain your own wellness practices.)
- Practice using body scans and deep breathing. (There's apps for that!)
- <u>Always: Collaboration, Creativity, Consent</u>

CORE IDEAS

Value embodiment

Validate sexual experience
(embracing paradox and parts)

Reduce shame and
increase belonging

Support self-identification

Build self-awareness

Develop resilience

Cultivate curiosity

Seek out embodied connections
(follow your yum!)

Increase leadership/
sense of agency

PLEASURE IS PERSONAL

THE PERSONAL IS THE POLITICAL

PLEASURE IS POLITICAL

The body cannot hold onto discomfort/danger and calm/pleasure at the exact same time.

The qualities of flexibility, adaptability, and creativity lead to survival, increased connections, and new possibilities.

"THE MASTER'S TOOLS WILL NEVER DISMANTLE THE MASTER'S HOUSE"

Practices of Connection	Practice of Oppression
Empathy	Intolerance/indifference
Appreciative inquiry	Ignoring systems of oppression
Radical inclusion	Weaponized pain
Power-with	Power-over
Vulnerability	Minimizing, dismissiveness, disdain & contempt
Strong but flexible boundaries	
Physical and emotional affection (consensual)	Manipulation & emotional fragility
Healing justice	Physical/emotional violence
	Carceral "justice"/punishment

SYMPTOMS OF TRAUMA*

<u>Hyperarousal</u>	<u>Hypo-arousal</u>
Hypervigilance	Diffuse boundaries
Rigid boundaries	Crying
Crying	Dissociation
Impulsivity/reactivity	Lack of eye contact
Labile	Withdrawal
Sudden anger	Underreacting
Undereating	Overeating
Substance use	Suicidal ideation
Flashbacks	Substance use
The past is alive	Chronic sense of shame/guilt
	Persistent sadness
	The past is alive

These are examples and this is not meant to be an exhaustive list.

INDICATORS OF WELLNESS (GREEN ZONE)

Bright eyes

Dynamic eye contact

Reaching out

Expressions of consent/boundaries/interest

Ability to initiate and/or receive contact

Creativity

Playfulness

Present is alive

ELEMENTS OF THE EROTIC

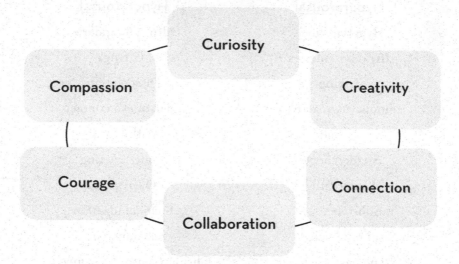

Additional Resources

APPS

Liberate App, a meditation app for the BIPOC community
liberatemeditation.com

The Tapping Solution for Emotional Freedom Technique (EFT)
thetappingsolutionapp.com

BOOKS

All About Love by bell hooks

The Come as You Are Workbook: A Practical Guide to the Science of Sex by Emily Nagoski, PhD

Emergent Strategy: Shaping Change, Changing Worlds by adrienne maree brown

Enjoy Sex (How, When and IF You Want To): A Practical and Inclusive Guide by Meg-John Barker and Justin Hancock

Healing Sex by Staci Haines

Pleasure Activism: The Politics of Feeling Good by adrienne maree brown

The Power of Neurodiversity: Unleashing the Advantages of Your Differently Wired Brain by Thomas Armstrong, PhD

Sexuality and the Black Church: A Womanist Perspective by Kelly Brown Douglas

WEBSITES

Afrosexology

Created by Dalychia and Rafaella, Afrosexology believes that "reclaiming and having agency over our bodies will transfer to other aspects of our lives and incite us to reclaim political, economic, and social agency." In addition to robust social media content, they offer a range of workshops and virtual events.

afrosexology.com

ANTE UP!

A powerful and revolutionary collective, ANTE UP! is creating the next generation of innovative sexuality therapists and educators through their trainings and professional development courses. If you are in the sexuality field or want to learn about and experience community-change work, sign up for any of their phenomenal opportunities.

anteuppd.com

BlackLine

Founded with a focus on Black femme LGBTQ folks, BlackLine is passionately committed to social justice with a two-pronged approach: they offer crisis counseling and collect information on negative police contact/police brutality.

callblackline.com

Inclusive Therapists

Inclusive Therapists is an online directory for mental health therapists of color and BIPOC clients to find one another.

inclusivetherapists.com

Modern Path

Modern Path is the brainchild of therapist and trainer Nick Fuentes. Modern Path offers psychotherapy and high-quality virtual trainings and is a hub for excellent info on gender, sexuality, relationship structure minorities (GSRM).

modernpath.net

National Queer and Trans Therapists of Color Network

NQTTCN is a national organization by and for queer and trans people of color (QTPoC). They have a directory for clients to find QTPoC therapists and also provide healing justice trainings and retreats.
nqttcn.com

MEDIA

Kimchi Cuddles

A humorous and touching comic about polyamory, queer, and gender-queer issues.
kimchicuddles.com

PODCASTS

Disability After Dark with Andrew Gurza

A unique glimpse into sex and disability, the fun found in sex and disability, and vulnerability around sex and disability through stories and conversations, hosted by Disability Awareness Consultant Andrew Gurza.
andrewgurza.com/podcast

The Confessional with Nadia Bolz-Weber

Guests share stories about difficult times with former stand-up comic, recovering alcoholic, pastor and founder of House for All Sinners and Saints, an inclusive, queer-friendly church. Like Nadia's books and sermons, the podcast is rich with empathy and humor and especially wonderful for anyone with a Christian upbringing.
nadiabolzweber.com/podcast

Finding Our Way with Prentis Hemphill

Conversations between Prentis Hemphill, somatics practitioner, movement facilitator, and coach, with activists, artists, and leaders on ways to realize the world we desire through personal healing and transformation, delving into topics such as embodiment, boundaries, harm, and creativity. (Prentis also maintains a wonderful blog.)
prentishemphill.com

Latinx Therapy

Adriana Alejandre, LMFT, explores mental health topics related to Latinx individuals in an effort to "demystify myths and diagnoses and address commonly stigmatized themes," with Latinx mental health professionals, entrepreneurs, and more. Includes bimonthly Spanish segments.
latinxtherapy.com/podcast

Trauma Queen

A miniseries hosted by Jimanekia Eborn, a queer media consultant, sex educator, and sexual assault and trauma expert. Includes conversations with survivors, therapists, partners, educators, and experts, all aimed at normalizing talking about assault and providing healing resources and steps forward for survivors and allies.
traumaqueen.love/trauma-queen

WEBINARS

Navigating Roadblocks of Sexual Pleasure by Hill Psychological and Consultation Services, led by sex therapists Dr. LaWanda Hill, Dr. Nikki Coleman, and Dr. Ebony
gumroad.com/l/CAvpAg

SOCIAL MEDIA

Instagram

Minaa B, LMSW: @minaa_b

The Nap Ministry: @thenapministry

SEEK Safely Inc.: @seeksafely

Sex Positive Families: @sexpositive_families

Shadeen Francis, LMFT: @shadeenfrancislmft

Trans Lifeline: @translifeline

Twitter

BIPOC Collective: @bipoc_aic

National Eating Disorders Association: @NEDAstaff

The Nap Ministry: @TheNapMinistry

The Trauma & Mental Health Report: @TraumaReport

Trevor Project: @TrevorProject

Notes

About This Book
in some cases, adding trigger warnings: Mevagh Sanson, Deryn Strange, and Maryanne Garry, "Trigger Warnings Are Trivially Helpful at Reducing Negative Affect, Intrusive Thoughts, and Avoidance," *Clinical Psychological Science* 7, no. 4 (March 4, 2019): 778–793, https://doi.org/10.1177/2167702619827018.

1 "Why Is This Happening to Me?"
painful childhood wounds open wide: Wendy Malt, *The Sexual Healing Journey: A Guide for Survivors of Sexual Abuse,* 3rd ed. (New York: William Morrow Paperbacks, 2012).

2 "What Is Happening to Me?"
The more recently identified fawn response: Pete Walker, "Emotional Flashback Management in the Treatment of Complex PTSD," Psychotherapy 2009 newsletter, https://www.psychotherapy.net/article/complex-ptsd.

All of this can lead to or heighten trauma: Substance Abuse and Mental Health Services Administration (US), *Trauma-Informed Care in Behavioral Health Services* (Rockville: SAMHSA [US], 2014), chap. 3, https://www.ncbi.nlm.nih.gov/books/NBK207191.

Sexual dysfunction, such as fearing arousal: Ateret Gewirtz-Meydan and Yael Lahav, "Sexual Dysfunction and Distress Among Childhood Sexual Abuse Survivors: The Role of Post-Traumatic Stress Disorder," *The Journal of Sexual Medicine* 17, no. 11 (2020): 2267–2278, https://doi.org/10.1016/j.jsxm.2020.07.016.

Creating or listening to music, dancing: Nan J. Wise, Eleni Frangos, and Barry R. Komisaruk, "Brain Activity Unique to Orgasm in Women: An fMRI Analysis," *The Journal of Sexual Medicine* 14, no. 11 (October 2017): 1380–1391, https://doi.org/10.1016/j .jsxm.2017.08.014; Nora Landis-Shack, Adrienne J. Heinz, Marcel O. Bonn-Miller, "Music Therapy for Posttraumatic Stress in Adults: A Theoretical Review" *Psychomusicology* 27, no. 4 (2017): 334–342, https://www.ncbi.nlm.nih.gov/pmc/articles /PMC5744879.

From a sex standpoint, orgasm: Gert Holstege et al., "Brain Activation During Human Male Ejaculation," *Journal of Neuroscience* 23, no. 27 (October 2003): 9185–9193, https://doi.org/10.1523/JNEUROSCI.23-27-09185.2003.

Research conducted at Widener University: Dulcinea Pitagora, "No Pain, No Gain?: Therapeutic and Relational Benefits of Subspace in BDSM Contexts," *Journal of Positive Sexuality* 3, no. 3 (2017): 44–54, https://journalofpositivesexuality.org/wp-content /uploads/2017/10/No-Pain-No-Gain-Therapeutic-and-Relational-Benefits-of -Subspace-in-BDSM-Pitagora.pdf.

3 "How Can I Stop This?"
White supremacy–fueled fat phobia: Sabrina Strings. *Fearing the Black Body: The Racial Origins of Fat Phobia.* (New York: NYU Press, 2017).

The Adverse Childhood Experiences: "Preventing Adverse Childhood Experiences," Centers for Disease Control and Prevention, https://www.cdc.gov/violenceprevention/aces /fastfact.html.

4 "I Need Help"

The same mindfulness practice or talk: Jennifer Huberty et al., "Relationship Between Mindfulness and Post-Traumatic Stress in Women Who Experienced Stillbirth," *Journal of Obstetric, Gynecologic, and Neonatal Nursing* 47, no. 6 (2018): 760–770.

This form of therapy is considered by many: Delphine-Émilie Bourdon et al., "Schemas and Coping Strategies in Cognitive-Behavioral Therapy for PTSD: A Systematic Review," *European Journal of Trauma, and Dissociation* 3, no. 1 (2019): 33–47, https://doi .org/10.1016/j.ejtd.2018.09.005.

Psychodynamic group therapy: Leonardo M. Leiderman, "Psychodynamic Group Therapy with Hispanic Migrants: Interpersonal, Relational Constructs in Treating Complex Trauma, Dissociation, and Enactments," *International Journal of Group Psychotherapy* 70, no. 2 (December 2019): 162–182, https://doi.org/10.1080/00207284.2019.1686 704.

Art therapy and music therapy can: American Music Therapy Association, *Music Therapy in Response to Crisis and Trauma*, https://www.musictherapy.org/assets/1/7/MT _Crisis_2006.pdf.

Therapy animals may also be an option: Johanna Lass-Hennemann et al., "Therapy Dogs as a Crisis Intervention After Traumatic Events? – An Experimental Study," *Frontiers in Psychology* 9 (September 2018): 1627, https://doi.org/10.3389/fpsyg.2018.01627.

A case study showed its benefits for reducing: Lucas Elms et al., "Cannabidiol in the Treatment of Post-Traumatic Stress Disorder: A Case Series." *Journal of Alternative and Complementary Medicine* 25, no. 4 (April 2019): https://doi.org/10.1089 /acm.2018.0437.

can interact with certain medications: Peter Grinspoon, "Cannabidiol (CBD) – What We Know and What We Don't," *Harvard Health Blog, Harvard Health Publishing*, August 24, 2018, https://www.health.harvard.edu/blog/cannabidiol-cbd-what-we-know-and -what-we-dont-2018082414476.

harmful minority of practitioners: F. Robin, J. Bonamy, and E. Ménétrier, "Hypnosis and False Memories," *Psychology of Consciousness: Theory, Research, and Practice* 5, no. 4 (2018): 358–373, https://doi.org/10.1037/cns0000150.

It's important to note that people of color: Timothy I. Michaels, "Inclusion of People of Color in Psychedelic-Assisted Psychotherapy: A Review of the Literature," *BMC Psychiatry* 18, no. 245 (July 2018), https://doi.org/10.1186/s12888-018-1824-6.

autism is often overlooked or diagnosed: David S. Mandell et al., "Racial/Ethnic Disparities in the Identification of Children with Autism Spectrum Disorders," *American Journal of Public Health* 99, no. 3 (March 2009): 493–498, https://doi.org/10.2105 /AJPH.2007.131243.

not to mention culturally appropriated: Traditional sweat lodges are safely used by Indigenous people in Sedona, who later sued James Arthur Ray for "desecration of a sacred Lakota ceremony."

5 "I Am Such a Problem."

Psychologist Russell Barkley: Allison Inserro, "Psychologist Barkley Says Life Expectancy Slashed in Worst Cases for Those With ADHD," *American Journal of Managed Care*, January 14, 2018, https://www.ajmc.com/view/psychologist-barkley-says-life -expectancy-slashed-in-worst-cases-for-those-with-adhd.

"irreparable harm can befall adults": Russel Barkley, "My Brother Died in a Car Crash Because of His ADHD," *ADDitude Magazine*, Fall 2012, https://www.additudemag .com/car-accidents-personal-essay-adult-adhd.

As Edward Hallowell, MD: Edward Hallowell, "Overcoming My ADHD Shame," updated July 30, 2019, in *ADHD Experts Podcast*, produced by *ADDitude Magazine*, podcast, https://www.additudemag.com/podcast-adhd-shame-edward-hallowell-md.

6 "Healing Is Taking Too Long."
statistics show that nearly twenty: "National Statistics," National Coalition Against Domestic Violence, 2020, https://ncadv.org/statistics.

7 "They Don't Understand."
For many, many years, extremely little: Matthew J. Friedman, "History of PTSD in Veterans: Civil War to DSM-5," PTSD: National Center for PTSD, U.S. Department of Veterans Affairs, 2019, https://www.ptsd.va.gov/understand/what/history_ptsd.asp.
like many people with borderline: "Causes of Borderline Personality Disorder," Bridges to Recovery, 2020, https://www.bridgestorecovery.com/borderline-personality-disorder/causes-of-borderline-personality-disorder.

8 "How Can I Get My Life Back?"
Post-traumatic growth is a theory: Lorna Collier, "Growth After Trauma: Why Are Some People More Resilient Than Others—And Can It Be Taught?," *Monitor on Psychology* 47, no. 10 (November 2016): 48, https://www.apa.org/monitor/2016/11/growth-trauma.
hypnotherapy, a methodology: Siobhan K. O'Toole, Shelby L. Solomon, and Stephen A. Bergdahl, "A Meta Analysis of Hypnotherapeutic Techniques in the Treatment of PTSD Symptoms," *Journal of Traumatic Stress* 29, no. 1 (February 2016): 97–100, https://doi.org/10.1002/jts.22077.
lack of thorough investigation: Allison Leota. "I Was a Sex-Crimes Prosecutor. Here's Why 'He Said, She Said' Is a Myth," *Time*, October 3, 2018, https://time.com/5413814/he-said-she-said-kavanaugh-ford-mitchell.
stemmed from vaginismus: "Vaginismus Typical Causes: The Internal Alarm," Vaginismus.com, https://www.vaginismus.com/causes-of-vaginismus.

9 "Should I Forgive? If So, How?"
"the capacity to deeply listen": Prentiss Hemphill, "On Healing," *Prentiss Hemphill* (blog), May 8, 2018, https://prentishemphill.com/blog/2018/5/8/on-healing-1.

10 "Dang. I Thought I Was Healed."
Given that boys and men: Patrizia Riccardi, "Male Rape: The Silent Victim and the Gender of the Listener." *Primary Care Companion to the Journal of Clinical Psychiatry* 12, no 6 (2010), https://www.ncbi.nlm.nih.gov/pmc/articles/PMC3067991.

About the Authors

August McLaughlin is a nationally recognized health and sexuality writer, trauma-informed certified sex educator, and host and producer of the podcast *Girl Boner Radio*. Her articles have been featured by *Cosmopolitan*, the *Washington Post*, *Salon*, *HuffPost*, LIVESTRONG .com, and more. She is the author of *Girl Boner: The Good Girl's Guide to Sexual Empowerment*, featured in the *New York Times*, *Health*, and *Shape*. She has presented at colleges, recovery centers, and the Centers for Disease Control and Prevention headquarters in Atlanta.

Jamila Dawson, LMFT, is a licensed sex and relationship therapist, writer, and educator. She runs her private psychotherapy and consulting business, Fire & Flow Therapy, and teaches as adjunct faculty at Antioch University Los Angeles. She has lectured at the University of Southern California and AASECT Summer Institute, and collaborated with a variety of sex therapists and educators, as well as *Buzzfeed*, *Playboy*, *Harper's Bazaar*, and other media outlets. She presents locally and nationally on sexuality, empowerment, BDSM/ kink, pleasure, relationships, and trauma-informed/healing-focused psychotherapy.